Manoeuvring by Maria Edgeworth

Maria Edgeworth was born at Black Bourton, Oxfordshire on January 1st 1768. Her early years were with her mother's family in England. Sadly, her mother died when Maria was five.

Maria was educated at Mrs Lattafière's school in Derby in 1775. There she studied dancing, French and other subjects. Maria transferred to Mrs Devis's school in Upper Wimpole Street, London. Her father began to focus more attention on Maria in 1781 when she nearly lost her sight to an eye infection.

She returned home to Ireland at 14 and took charge of her younger siblings. She herself was home-tutored by her father in Irish economics and politics, science, literature and law. Despite her youth literature was in her blood. Maria also became her father's assistant in managing the family's large Edgeworthstown estate.

Maria first published 1795 with 'Letters for Literary Ladies'. That same year 'An Essay on the Noble Science of Self-Justification', written for a female audience, advised women on how to obtain better rights in general and specifically from their husbands.

'Practical Education' (1798) is a progressive work on education. Maria's ambition was to create an independent thinker who understands the consequences of his or her actions.

Her first novel, 'Castle Rackrent' was published anonymously in 1800 without her father's knowledge. It was an immediate success and firmly established Maria's appeal to the public.

Her father married four times and the last of these to Frances, a year younger and a confidante of Maria, who pushed them to travel more widely: London, Britain and Europe were all now visited.

The second series of 'Tales of Fashionable Life' (1812) did so well that she was now the most commercially successful novelist of her age.

She particularly worked hard to improve the living standards of the poor in Edgeworthstown and to provide schools for the local children of all and any denomination.

After a visit to see her relations Maria had severe chest pains and died suddenly of a heart attack in Edgeworthstown on 22nd May 1849. She was 81.

Index of Contents

MANOEUVRING

CHAPTER I

*"And gave her words, where oily Flatt'ry lays
The pleasing colours of the art of praise."*
—*PARNELL.*

NOTE FROM MRS. BEAUMONT TO MISS WALSINGHAM

"I am more grieved than I can express, my dearest Miss Walsingham, by a cruel contre-temps, which must prevent my indulging myself in the long-promised and long-expected pleasure of being at your fête de famille on Tuesday, to celebrate your dear father's birthday. I trust, however, to your conciliating goodness, my kind young friend, to represent my distress properly to Mr. Walsingham. Make him sensible, I conjure you, that my heart is with you all, and assure him that this is no common apology. Indeed, I never employ such artifices with my friends: to them, and to you in particular, my dear, I always speak with perfect frankness and candour. Amelia, with whom, entre nous, you are more a favourite than ever, is so much vexed and mortified by this disappointment, that I see I shall not be restored to favour till I can fix a day for going to you: yet when that may be, circumstances, which I should not feel myself quite justified in mentioning, will not permit me to decide.

"Kindest regards and affectionate remembrances to all your dear circle.—Any news of the young captain? Any hopes of his return from sea?

"Ever with perfect truth, my dearest Miss Walsingham's sincere friend,

"EUGENIA BEAUMONT.

"P.S.—Private—read to yourself.

"To be candid with you, my dear young friend, my secret reason for denying myself the pleasure of Tuesday's fête is, that I have just heard that there is a shocking chicken-pox in the village near you; and I confess it is one of my weaknesses to dread even the bare rumour of such a thing, on account of my

Amelia: but I should not wish to have this mentioned in your house, because you must be sensible your father would think it an idle womanish fear; and you know how anxious I am for his esteem.

"Burn this, I beseech you—

"Upon second thoughts, I believe it will be best to tell the truth, and the whole truth, to your father, if you should see that nothing else will do—In short, I write in haste, and must trust now, as ever, entirely to your discretion."

"Well, my dear," said Mr. Walsingham to his daughter, as the young lady sat at the breakfast table looking over this note, "how long do you mean to sit the picture of The Delicate Embarrassment? To relieve you as far as in me lies, let me assure you that I shall not ask to see this note of Mrs. Beaumont's, which as usual seems to contain some mighty mystery."

"No great mystery; only—"

"Only—some minikin mystery?" said Mr. Walsingham. "Yes, 'Elle est politique pour des choux et des raves.'—This charming widow Beaumont is manoeuvrer.1 We can't well make an English word of it. The species, thank Heaven! is not so numerous yet in England as to require a generic name. The description, however, has been touched by one of our poets:

'Julia's a manager: she's born for rule, And knows her wiser husband is a fool. For her own breakfast she'll project a scheme, Nor take her tea without a stratagem.'

Even from the time when Mrs. Beaumont was a girl of sixteen I remember her manoeuvring to gain a husband, and then manoeuvring to manage him, which she did with triumphant address."

"What sort of a man was Colonel Beaumont?"

"An excellent man; an open-hearted soldier, of the strictest honour and integrity."

"Then is it not much in Mrs. Beaumont's favour, that she enjoyed the confidence of such a man, and that he left her guardian to his son and daughter?"

"If he had lived with her long enough to become acquainted with her real character, what you say, my dear, would be unanswerable. But Colonel Beaumont died a few years after his marriage, and during those few years he was chiefly with his regiment."

"You will, however, allow," said Miss Walsingham, "that since his death Mrs. Beaumont has justified his confidence.—Has she not been a good guardian, and an affectionate mother?"

"Why—as a guardian, I think she has allowed her son too much liberty, and too much money. I have heard that young Beaumont has lost a considerable sum at Newmarket. I grant you that Mrs. Beaumont is an affectionate mother, and I am convinced that she is extremely anxious to advance the worldly interests of her children; still I cannot, my dear, agree with you, that she is a good mother. In the whole course of the education of her son and daughter, she has pursued a system of artifice. Whatever she wanted them to learn, or to do, or to leave undone, some stratagem, sentimental or scenic, was employed; somebody was to hint to some other body to act upon Amelia to make her do so and so.

Nothing—that is, nothing like truth, ever came directly from the mother: there were always whisperings and mysteries, and 'Don't say that before Amelia!' and 'I would not have this told to Edward,' because it might make him like something that she did not wish that he should like, and that she had her reasons for not letting him know that she did not wish him to like. There was always some truth to be concealed for some mighty good purpose; and things and persons were to be represented in false lights, to produce on some particular occasion some partial effect. All this succeeded admirably in detail, and for the management of helpless, ignorant, credulous childhood. But mark the consequences of this system: children grow up, and cannot always see, hear, and understand, just as their mothers please. They will go into the world; they will mix with others; their eyes will be opened; they will see through the whole system of artifice by which their childhood was so cleverly managed; and then, confidence in the parent must be destroyed for ever."

Miss Walsingham acknowledged the truth of what her father said; but she observed that this was a common error in education, which had the sanction of high authority in its favour; even the eloquent Rousseau, and the elegant and ingenious Madame de Genlis. "And it is certain," continued Miss Walsingham, "that Mrs. Beaumont has not made her children artful; both Amelia and Mr. Beaumont are remarkably open, sincere, honourable characters. Mr. Beaumont, indeed, carries his sincerity almost to a fault: he is too blunt, perhaps, in his manner;—and Amelia, though she is of such a timid, gentle temper, and so much afraid of giving pain, has always courage enough to speak the truth, even in circumstances where it is most difficult. So at least you must allow, my dear father, that Mrs. Beaumont has made her children sincere."

"I am sorry, my dear, to seem uncharitable; but I must observe, that sometimes the very faults of parents produce a tendency to opposite virtues in their children: for the children suffer by the consequences of these faults, and detecting, despise, and resolve to avoid them. As to Amelia and Mr. Beaumont, their acquaintance with our family has been no unfavourable circumstance in their education. They saw amongst us the advantages of sincerity: they became attached to you, and to my excellent ward Captain Walsingham; he obtained strong power over young Beaumont's mind, and used it to the best purposes. Your friendship for Amelia was, I think, equally advantageous to her: as you are nearly of the same age, you had opportunities of winning her confidence; and your stronger mind fortified hers, and inspired her timid character with the courage necessary to be sincere."

"Well," persisted Miss Walsingham, "though Mrs. Beaumont may have used a little finesse towards her children in trifles, yet in matters of consequence, I do think that she has no interest but theirs; and her affection for them will make her lay aside all art, when their happiness is at stake."

Mr. Walsingham shook his head.—"And do you then really believe, my dear Marianne, that Mrs. Beaumont would consider any thing, for instance, in the marriage of her son and daughter, but fortune, and what the world calls connexion and establishments?"

"Certainly I cannot think that these are Mrs. Beaumont's first objects; because we are people but of small fortune, and yet she prefers us to many of large estates and higher station."

"You should say, she professes to prefer us," replied Mr. Walsingham. "And do you really believe her to be sincere? Now, there is my ward, Captain Walsingham, for whom she pretends to have such a regard, do you think that Mrs. Beaumont wishes her daughter should marry him?"

"I do, indeed; but Mrs. Beaumont must speak cautiously on that subject; this is prudence, not dissimulation: for you know that my cousin Walsingham never declared his attachment to Miss Beaumont; on the contrary, he always took the most scrupulous pains to conceal it from her, because he had not fortune enough to marry, and he was too honourable to attempt, or even to wish, to engage the affections of one to whom he had no prospect of being united."

"He is a noble fellow!" exclaimed Mr. Walsingham. "There is no sacrifice of pleasure or interest he would hesitate to make to his duty. For his friends there is no exertion, no endurance, no forbearance, of which he has not shown himself capable. For his country—All I ask from Heaven for him is, opportunity to serve his country. Whether circumstances, whether success, will ever prove his merits to the world, I cannot foretell; but I shall always glory in him as my ward, my relation, my friend."

"Mrs. Beaumont speaks of him just as you do," said Miss Walsingham.

"Speaks, but not thinks," said Mr. Walsingham. "No, no! Captain Walsingham is not the man she desires for a son-in-law. She wants to marry Amelia to Sir John Hunter."

"To Sir John Hunter!"

"Yes, to Sir John Hunter, a being without literature, without morals, without even youth, to plead in his favour. He is nearly forty years old, old enough to be Amelia's father; yet this is the man whom Mrs. Beaumont prefers for the husband of her beloved daughter, because he is heir presumptive to a great estate, and has the chance of a reversionary earldom.—And this is your modern good mother."

"Oh, no, no!" cried Miss Walsingham, "you do Mrs. Beaumont injustice; I assure you she despises Sir John Hunter as much as we do."

"Yet observe the court she has paid to the whole family of the Hunters."

"Yes, but that has been merely from regard to the late Lady Hunter, who was her particular friend."

"Particular friend! a vamped-up, sentimental conversation reason."

"But I assure you," persisted Miss Walsingham, "that I know Mrs. Beaumont's mind better than you do, father, at least on this subject."

"You! a girl of eighteen, pretend to know a manoeuvrer of her age!"

"Only let me tell you my reasons.—It was but last week that Mrs. Beaumont told me that she did not wish to encourage Sir John Hunter, and that she should be perfectly happy if she could see Amelia united to such a man as Captain Walsingham."

"Such a man as Captain Walsingham! nicely guarded expression!"

"But you have not heard all yet.—Mrs. Beaumont anxiously inquired from me whether he had made any prize-money, whether there was any chance of his returning soon; and she added, with particular emphasis, 'You don't know how much I wish it! You don't know what a favourite he is of mine!'"

"That last, I will lay any wager," cried Mr. Walsingham, "she said in a whisper, and in a corner."

"Yes, but she could not do otherwise, for Amelia was present. Mrs. Beaumont took me aside."

"Aside; ay, ay, but take care, I advise you, of her asides, and her whisperings, and her cornerings, and her inuendoes, and semiconfidences, lest your own happiness, my dear, unsuspecting, enthusiastic daughter, should be the sacrifice."

Miss Walsingham now stood perfectly silent, in embarrassed and breathless anxiety.

"I see," continued her father, "that Mrs. Beaumont, for whose mighty genius one intrigue at a time is not sufficient, wants also to persuade you, my dear, that she wishes to have you for a daughter-in-law: and yet all the time she is doing every thing she can to make her son marry that fool, Miss Hunter, merely because she has two hundred thousand pounds fortune."

"There I can assure you that you are mistaken," said Miss Walsingham; "Mrs. Beaumont dreads that her son should marry Miss Hunter. Mrs. Beaumont thinks her as silly as you do, and complained to me of her having no taste for literature, or for any thing, but dress, and trifling conversation."

"I wonder, then, that Mrs. Beaumont selects her continually for her companion."

"She thinks Miss Hunter the most insipid companion in the world; but I dare not tell you, lest you should laugh at me again, that it was for the sake of the late Lady Hunter that Mrs. Beaumont was so kind to the daughter; and now Miss Hunter is so fond of her, and so grateful, that, as Mrs. Beaumont says, it would be cruelty to shake her off."

"Mighty plausible! But the truth of all this, begging Mrs. Beaumont's pardon, I doubt; I will not call it a falsehood, but I may be permitted to call it a Beaumont. Time will show: and in the mean time, my dear daughter, be on your guard against Mrs. Beaumont's art, and against your own credulity. The momentary pain I give my friends by speaking the plain truth, I have always found overbalanced by the pleasure and advantage of mutual confidence. Our domestic happiness has arisen chiefly from our habits of openness and sincerity. Our whole souls are laid open; there is no management, no 'intrigue de cabinet, no 'esprit de la ligue.'"

Mr. Walsingham now left the room; and Miss Walsingham, absorbed in reflections more interesting to her than even the defence of Mrs. Beaumont, went out to walk. Her father's house was situated in a beautiful part of Devonshire, near the sea-shore, in the neighbourhood of Plymouth; and as Miss Walsingham was walking on the beach, she saw an old fisherman mooring his boat to the projecting stump of a tree. His figure was so picturesque, that she stopped to sketch it; and as she was drawing, a woman came from the cottage near the shore to ask the fisherman what luck he had had. "A fine turbot," says he, "and a john-doree."

"Then away with them this minute to Beaumont Park," said the woman; "for here's Madam Beaumont's man, Martin, called in a flustrum while you was away, to say madam must have the nicest of our fish, whatsomever it might be, and a john-doree, if it could be had for love or money, for Tuesday."—Here the woman, perceiving Miss Walsingham, dropped a curtsy. "Your humble servant, Miss Walsingham," said the woman.

"On Tuesday?" said Miss Walsingham: "are you sure that Mrs. Beaumont bespoke the fish for Tuesday?"

"Oh, sartin sure, miss; for Martin mentioned, moreover, what he had heard talk in the servants' hall, that there is to be a very pettiklar old gentleman, as rich! as rich! as rich can be! from foreign parts, and a great friend of the colonel that's dead; and he—that is, the old pettiklar gentleman—is to be down all the way from Lon'on to dine at the park on Tuesday for sartin: so, husband, away with the john-doree and the turbot, while they be fresh."

"But why," thought Miss Walsingham, "did not Mrs. Beaumont tell us the plain truth, if this is the truth?"

CHAPTER II

"Young Hermes next, a close contriving god,
Her brows encircled with his serpent rod;
Then plots and fair excuses fill her brain,
And views of breaking am'rous vows for gain."

The information which Mrs. Beaumont's man, Martin, had learned from the servants' hall, and had communicated to the fisherman's wife, was more correct, and had been less amplified, embellished, misunderstood, or misrepresented, than is usually found to be the case with pieces of news which are so heard and so repeated. It was true that Mrs. Beaumont expected to see on Tuesday an old gentleman, a Mr. Palmer, who had been a friend of her husband's; he had lately returned from Jamaica, where he had made a large fortune. It is true, also, that this old gentleman was a little particular, but not precisely in the sense in which the fisherman's wife understood the phrase; he was not particularly fond of john-dorees and turbots, but he was particularly fond of making his fellow-creatures happy; particularly generous, particularly open and honest in his nature, abhorring all artifice himself, and unsuspicious of it in others. He was unacquainted with Mrs. Beaumont's character, as he had been for many years in the West Indies, and he knew her only from her letters, in which she appeared every thing that was candid and amiable. His great friendship for her deceased husband also inclined him to like her. Colonel Beaumont had appointed him one of the guardians of his children, but Mr. Palmer, being absent from England, had declined to act: he was also trustee to Mrs. Beaumont's marriage-settlement, and she had represented that it was necessary he should be present at the settlement of her family affairs upon her son's coming of age; an event which was to take place in a few days. The urgent representations of Mrs. Beaumont, and the anxious desire she expressed to see Mr. Palmer, had at last prevailed with the good old gentleman to journey down to Beaumont Park, though he was a valetudinarian, and though he was obliged, he said, to return to Jamaica with the West India fleet, which was expected to sail in ten days; so that he announced positively that he could stay but a week at Beaumont Park with his good friends and relations.

He was related but distantly to the Beaumonts, and he stood in precisely the same degree of relationship to the Walsinghams. He had no other relations, and his fortune was completely at his own disposal. On this fortune our cunning widow had speculated long and deeply, though in fact there was no occasion for art: it was Mr. Palmer's intention to leave his large fortune to the Beaumonts; or to divide it between the Beaumont and Walsingham families; and had she been sincere in her professed desire of a complete union by a double marriage between the representatives of the families, her favourite object would have been, in either case, equally secure. Here was a plain, easy road to her object; but it was too direct for Mrs. Beaumont. With all her abilities, she could never comprehend the axiom that a right line is the shortest possible line between any two points:—an axiom equally true in morals and in mathematics. No, the serpentine line was, in her opinion, not only the most beautiful, but the most expeditious, safe, and convenient.

She had formed a triple scheme of such intricacy, that it is necessary distinctly to state the argument of her plot, lest the action should be too complicated to be easily developed.

She had, in the first place, a design of engrossing the whole of Mr. Palmer's fortune for her own family; and for this purpose she determined to prevent Mr. Palmer from becoming acquainted with his other relations, the Walsinghams, to whom she had always had a secret dislike, because they were of remarkably open, sincere characters. As Mr. Palmer proposed to stay but a week in the country, this scheme of preventing their meeting seemed feasible.

In the second place, Mrs. Beaumont wished to marry her daughter to Sir John Hunter, because Sir John was heir expectant to a large estate, called the Wigram estate, and because there was in his family a certain reversionary title, the earldom of Puckeridge, which would devolve to Sir John after the death of a near relation.

In the third place, Mrs. Beaumont wished to marry her own son to Miss Hunter, who was Sir John's sister by a second marriage, and above twenty years younger than he was: this lady was preferred to Miss Walsingham for a daughter-in-law, for the reasons which Mr. Walsingham had given; because she possessed an independent fortune of two hundred thousand pounds, and because she was so childish and silly that Mrs. Beaumont thought she could always manage her easily, and by this means retain power over her son. Miss Hunter was very pretty, and Mrs. Beaumont had observed that her son had sometimes been struck with her beauty sufficiently to give hopes that, by proper management, he might be diverted from his serious, sober preference of Miss Walsingham.

Mrs. Beaumont foresaw many difficulties in the execution of these plans. She knew that Amelia liked Captain Walsingham, and that Captain Walsingham was attached to her, though he had never declared his love: and she dreaded that Captain Walsingham, who was at this time at sea, should return, just whilst Mr. Palmer was with her; because she was well aware that the captain was a kind of man Mr. Palmer would infinitely prefer to Sir John Hunter. Indeed, she had been secretly informed that Mr. Palmer hated every one who had a title; therefore she could not, whilst he was with her, openly encourage Sir John Hunter in his addresses to Amelia. To conciliate these seemingly incompatible schemes, she determined—But let our heroine speak for herself.

"My dearest Miss Hunter," said she, "now we are by ourselves, let me open my mind to you; I have been watching for an opportunity these two days, but so hurried as I have been!—Where's Amelia?"

"Out walking, ma'am. She told me you begged her to walk to get rid of her head-ache; and that she might look well to-day, as Mr. Palmer is to come. I would not go with her, because you whispered to me at breakfast that you had something very particular to say to me."

"But you did not give that as a reason, I hope! Surely you didn't tell Amelia that I had something particular to say to you?"

"Oh, no, ma'am; I told her that I had something to do about my dress—and so I had—my new hat to try on."

"True, my love; quite right; for you know I wouldn't have her suspect that we had any thing to say to each other that we didn't wish her to hear, especially as it is about herself."

"Herself!—Oh, is it?" said Miss Hunter, in a tone of disappointment.

"And about you, too, my darling. Be assured I have no daughter I love better, or ever shall. With such a son as I have, and such a daughter-in-law as I hope and trust I shall have ere long, I shall think myself the most fortunate of mothers."

Silly Miss Hunter's face brightened up again. "But now, my love," continued Mrs. Beaumont, taking her hand, leading her to a window, and speaking very low, though no one else was in the room, "before we talk any more of what is nearest my heart, I must get you to write a note for me to your brother, directly, for there is a circumstance I forgot—thoughtless creature that I am! but indeed, I never can think when I feel much. Some people are always so collected and prudent. But I have none of that!—Heigho! Well, my dear, you must supply my deficiencies. You will write and tell Sir John, that in my agitation when he made his proposal for my Amelia, of which I so frankly approved, I omitted to warn him, that no hint must be given that I do any thing more than permit him to address my daughter upon an equal footing with any other gentleman who might address her. Stay, my dear; you don't understand me, I see. In short, to be candid with you—old Mr. Palmer is coming to-day, you know. Now, my dear, you must be aware that it is of the greatest consequence to the interests of my family, of which I hope you always consider yourself (for I have always considered you) as forming a part, and a very distinguished part—I say, my darling, that we must consider that it is our interest in all things to please and humour this good old gentleman. He will be with us but for a week, you know. Well, the point is this. I have been informed from undoubted authority, people who were about him at the time, and knew, that the reason he quarrelled with that nephew of his, who died two years ago, was the young man's having accepted a baronetage: and at that time old Palmer swore, that no sprig of quality—those were the very words—should ever inherit a shilling of his money. Such a ridiculous whim! But these London merchants, who make great fortunes from nothing, are apt to have their little eccentricities; and then, they have so much pride in their own way, and so much self-will and mercantile downrightness in their manners, that there's no managing them but by humouring their fancies. I'm convinced, if Mr. Palmer suspected that I even wished Amelia to marry Sir John, he would never leave any of us a farthing, and it would all go to the Walsinghams. So, my dear, do you explain to your brother, that though I have not the least objection to his coming here whilst Mr. Palmer is with us, he must not take umbrage at any seeming coldness in my manner. He knows my heart, I trust; at least, you do, my Albina. And even if I should be obliged to receive or to go to see the Walsinghams, which, by-the-bye, I have taken means to prevent; but if it should happen that they were to hear of Palmer's being with us, and come, and Sir John should meet them, he must not be surprised or jealous at my speaking in the highest terms of Captain Walsingham. This I shall be obliged to do as a blind before Mr. Palmer. I must make him believe that I prefer a commoner for my son-in-law, or we are all undone with him. You know it is my son's interest, and yours, as well as your brother's and Amelia's, that I consider. So explain all this to him, my dear; you will explain it so much better, and make it so much more palpable to your brother than I could."

"Dear Mrs. Beaumont, how can you think so? You who write so well, and such long letters about every thing, and so quick! But goodness! I shall never get it all into a letter I'm afraid, and before Mr. Palmer comes, and then it will soon be dressing-time! La! I could say it all to John in five minutes: what a pity he is not here to-day!"

"Well, my love, then suppose you were to go to him; as you so prudently remark, things of this sort are always so much easier and better said than written. And now I look at my watch, I see you cannot have time to write a long letter, and to dress. So I believe, though I shall grieve to lose you, I must consent to your going for this one day to your brother's. My carriage and Williamson shall attend you," said Mrs. Beaumont, ringing the bell to order the carriage; "but remember you promise me now to come back, positively, to-morrow, or next day at farthest, if I should not be able to send the carriage again to-morrow. I would not, upon any account, have you away, if it can possibly be helped, whilst Mr. Palmer is here, considering you as I do [The carriage to the door directly, and Williamson to attend Miss Hunter]—considering you as I do, my dearest Albina, quite as my own daughter."

"Oh, my dearest Mrs. Beaumont, you are so kind!" said the poor girl, whom Mrs. Beaumont could always thus easily pay with words.

The carriage came to the door with such prompt obedience to Mrs. Beaumont's summons, that one of a more reflecting or calculating nature than Miss Hunter might have suspected that it had been ordered to be in readiness to carry her away this morning.

"Fare ye well, my own Albina! be sure you don't stay long from us," said Mrs. Beaumont, accompanying her to the hall-door. "A thousand kind things to everybody, and your brother in particular. But, my dear Miss Hunter, one word more," said she, following to the carriage door, and whispering: "there's another thing that I must trust to your management and cleverness;—I mentioned that Mr. Palmer was to know nothing of the approbation of Sir John's suit."

"Oh, yes, yes, ma'am, I understand perfectly."

"But stay, my love; you must understand, too, that it is to be quite a secret between ourselves, not to be mentioned to my son even; for you know he is sudden in his temper, and warm and quite in the Walsingham interest, and there's no knowing what might be the consequence if it were to be let out imprudently, and Sir John and Edward both so high-spirited. One can't be too cautious, my dear, to prevent mischief between gentlemen. So caution your brother to leave it to me to break it, and bring things about with Edward and Amelia,"—[stopping Miss Hunter again as she made a second effort to get into the carriage,]—"You comprehend, my dear, that Amelia is not in the secret yet—so not a word from your brother to her about my approbation!—that would ruin all. I trust to his honour; and besides—" drawing the young lady back for the third whisper.—Miss Hunter stood suspended with one foot in air, and the other on the step; the coachman, impatient to be off, manoeuvred to make his horses restless, whilst at the same time he cried aloud—"So! so! Prancer—stand still, Peacock; stand still, sir!"

Miss Hunter jumped down on terra firma. "Those horses frighten me so for you, my dear!" said Mrs. Beaumont. "Martin, stand at their heads. My dear child, I won't detain you, for you'll be late. I had only to say, that—oh! that I trust implicitly to your brother's honour; but, besides this, it will not be amiss for you to hint, as you know you can delicately—delicately, you understand—that it is for his interest to leave me to manage every thing. Yet none of this is to be said as if from me—pray don't let it come from me. Say it all from yourself. Don't let my name be mentioned at all. Don't commit me, you understand?"

"Perfectly, perfectly, ma'am: one kiss, dear Mrs. Beaumont, and adieu. Is my dressing-box in? Tell him to drive fast, for I hate going slow. Dearest Mrs. Beaumont, good bye. I feel as if I were going for an age, though it is only for one day."

"Dear, affectionate girl! I love heart—Good bye—Drive fast, as Miss Hunter desires you."

Our fair politician, well satisfied with the understanding of her confidante, which never comprehended more than met the ear, and secure in a chargé d'affaires, whose powers it was never necessary to limit, stood on the steps before the house-door, deep in reverie, for some minutes after the carriage had driven away, till she was roused by seeing her son returning from his morning's ride.

CHAPTER III

"Will you hear a Spanish lady,
How she woo'd an English man?
Garments gay as rich as may be,
Deck'd with jewels, she had on."
THE SPANISH LADY'S LOVE.
Percy's Reliques of Ancient Poetry

Mr. Beaumont had just been at a neighbouring farm-house, where there lived one of Mr. Walsingham's tenants; a man of the name of Birch, a respectable farmer, who was originally from Ireland, and whose son was at sea with Captain Walsingham. The captain had taken young Birch under his particular care, at Mr. Walsingham's request.

Birch's parents had this day received a letter from their son, which in the joy and pride of their hearts they showed to Mr. Beaumont, who was in the habit of calling at their house to inquire if they had heard any news of their son, or of Captain Walsingham. Mr. Beaumont liked to read Birch's letters, because they were written with characteristic simplicity and affection, and somewhat in the Irish idiom, which this young sailor's English education had not made him entirely forget.

LETTER FROM BIRCH TO HIS PARENTS.

"H.M.S. l'Ambuscade.

"HONOURED PARENTS,

"I write this from sea, lat. N. 44.15—long. W. 9.45—wind N.N.E.—to let you know you will not see me so soon as I said in my last, of the 16th. Yesterday, P.M. two o'clock, some despatches were brought to my good captain, by the Pickle sloop, which will to-morrow, wind and weather permitting, alter our destination. What the nature of them is I cannot impart to you, for it has not transpired beyond the lieutenants; but whatever I do under the orders of my good captain, I am satisfied and confident all is for the best. For my own share, I long for an opportunity of fighting the French, and of showing the captain what is in me, and that the pains he has took to make a gentleman, and an honour to his majesty's service, of me, is not thrown away. Had he been my own father, or brother, he could not be better, or done more. God willing, I will never disgrace his principles, for it would be my ambition to be like him in every respect; and he says, if I behave myself as I ought, I shall soon be a lieutenant; and a lieutenant in his majesty's navy is as good a gentleman as any in England, and has a right (tell my sister Kitty) to hand the first woman in Lon'on out of her carriage, if he pleases, and if she pleases.

"Now we talk of ladies, and as please God we shall soon be in action, and may not have another opportunity of writing to you this great while, for there is talk of our sailing southward with the fleet to bring the French and Spaniards to action, I think it best to send you all the news I have in this letter. But pray bid Kate, with my love, mind this, that not a word of the following is to take wind for her life, on account of my not knowing if it might be agreeable, or how it might affect my good captain, and others that shall be nameless. You must know then that when we were at —, where we were stationed six weeks and two days, waiting for the winds, and one cause or other, we used to employ ourselves, I and my captain, taking soundings (which I can't more particularly explain the nature of to you, especially in a letter); for he always took me out to attend him in preference to any other; and after he had completed his soundings, and had no farther use for me in that job, I asked him leave to go near the same place in the evening to fish, which my good captain consented to (as he always does to what (duty done) can gratify me), provided I was in my ship by ten. Now you must know that there are convents in this country (which you have often heard of, Kitty, no doubt), being damnable places, where young Catholic women are shut up unmarried, often, it is to be reasonably supposed, against their wills. And there is a convent in one of the suburbs which has a high back wall to the garden of it that comes down near the strand; and it was under this wall we two used to sound, and that afterwards I used to be fishing. And one evening, when I was not thinking of any such thing, there comes over the wall a huge nosegay of flowers, with a stone in it, that made me jump. And this for three evenings running the same way, about the same hour; till at last one evening as I was looking up at the wall, as I had now learned to do about the time the nosegays were thrown over, I saw coming down a stone tied to a string, and to the stone a letter, the words of which I can't particularly take upon me to recollect, because I gave up the paper to my captain, who desired it of me, and took no copy; but the sense was, that in that convent there was shut up a lady, the daughter of an English gentleman by a Spanish wife, both her parents being dead, and her Spanish relations and father-confessor (or catholic priest of a man), not wishing she should get to England, where she might be what she had a right to be by birth, at least by her father's side (a protestant), shut her up since she was a child. And that there was a relative of hers in England, who with a wicked lawyer or attorney had got possession of her estate, and made every body believe she was dead. And so, it being seven years and more since she was heard of, she is what is called dead in law, which sort of death however won't signify, if she appears again. Wherefore the letter goes on to say, she would be particularly glad to make her escape, and get over to old England. But she confesses that she is neither young nor handsome, and may-be never may be rich; therefore, that whoever helps her must do it for the sake of doing good and nothing else; for though she would pay all expenses handsomely, she could not promise more. And that she knew the danger of the undertaking to be great; greater for them that would carry her off even than for herself. That she knows, however, that British sailors are brave as they are generous (this part of the letter was very well indited, and went straight to my heart the minute ever I read it); and she wished it could be in the power of Captain Walsingham to take her under his immediate protection, and that she had taken measures so as she could escape over the wall of the garden if he would have a boat in readiness to carry her to his ship; and at the same hour next evening the stone should be let down as usual, and he might fasten his answer to it, which would be drawn up in due course. Concluding all this with, 'That she would not go at all unless Captain Walsingham came for her himself (certifying himself to be himself, I suppose), for she knew him to be a gentleman by reputation, and she should be safe under his protection, and so would her secret, she was confident, at all events.' This was the entire and sum total of the letter. So when I had read to the end, and looked for the postscript and all, I found for my pains that the lady mistook me for my captain, or would not have written or thrown the nosegays. So I took the letter to my captain; and what he answered, and how it was settled (by signals, I suppose) between them after, it was not for me to inquire. Not a word more was said by him to me or I to him on the topic, till the very night we were to sail for England. It was then that our captain took me aside, and he says, 'Birch, will you assist me? I ask this not as your captain, so you are at liberty to do as you please. Will you help me to rescue this lady, who seems to be unjustly detained, and to carry her back safe to her country and her friends?' I told him I would do that or any thing else he bid me, confident he would never ask me to do a wrong thing; and as to the lady, I should be proud to help to carry her off to old England and her lawful friends, only I thought (if I might be so bold) it was a pity she was not young and handsome, for his sake. At that he smiled, and only said, 'Perhaps it was best for him as it was.' Then he settled about the boat, and who were to go, and when. It was twelve o'clock striking by the great town clock when we were under the walls of the convent, as appointed. And all was hush and silent as the grave for our very lives. For it was a matter of life or death, I promise you, and we all knew as much, and the sailors had a dread of the Inquisition upon them that was beyond all terrible! So we watched and waited, and waited and watched so long, that we thought something must have gone wrong, or that all was found out, and the captain could not delay the ship's sailing; and he struck his repeater, and it was within a quarter of one, and he said, 'It is too late; we must put back.' Just then, I, that was watching with the lantern in my hand, gave notice, and first there comes down a white bundle, fastened to the stone and cord. Then the captain and I fixed the ladder of ropes, and down came the lady, as well as ever she went up, and not a word but away with her: the captain had her in a trice in our boat, safe and snug, and off we put, rowing for the bare life, all silent as ever. I think I hear the striking of our oars and the plashing of the water this minute, which we would have gladly silenced, but could not any way in nature. But none heard it, or at least took any notice against us. I can give you no idea of the terror which the lady manifested when the boat stood out to sea, at the slightest squall of wind, or the least agitation of the waves; for besides being naturally cowardly, as all or most women are for the first time at sea, here was a poor soul who had been watching, and may be fasting, and worn out mind and body with the terror of perfecting her escape from the convent, where she had been immured all her life, and as helpless as a child. So it was wonderful she went through it as well as she did and without screaming, which should be an example to Kate and others. Glad enough even we men were when we reached the ship. There was, at that time, a silence on board you could have heard a pin drop, all being in perfect readiness for getting under way, the sails ready for dropping, and officers and sailors waiting in the greatest expectation of our boat's return. Our boat passed swiftly alongside, and great beyond belief was the astonishment of all at seeing a woman veiled, hoisted out, and in, and ushered below, half fainting. I never felt more comfortable in my life than when we found her and ourselves safe aboard l'Ambuscade. The anchor was instantly weighed, all sail made, and the ship stood out to sea. To the lady the captain gave up his cabin: double sentries were placed, and as the captain ordered, every precaution that could shield her character in such suspicious circumstances were enforced with the utmost punctilio. I cannot describe, nor can you even conceive, Kate, the degree of curiosity shown about her; all striving to get a sight of her when she first went down, and most zealous they were to bring lights; but that would not do, for they could not see her for her veil. Yet through all we could make out that she was a fine figure of a woman at any rate, and something more than ordinary, from the air she had with her. The next day when she was sitting on deck the wind by times would blow aside her veil so as to give us glimpses of her face; when, to our surprise, and I am sure to the captain's satisfaction, we found she was beyond all contradiction young and handsome. And moreover I have reason to believe she has fine jewels with her, besides a ring from her own finger, which with a very pretty action she put on his, that next day on deck, as I noticed, when nobody was minding. So that no doubt she is as much richer as she is handsomer than she made believe, contrary to the ways of other women, which is in her favour and my good captain's; for from what I can judge, after all he has done for her, she has no dislike nor objection to him.

"I have not time to add any thing more, but my love to Kitty, and Nancy, and Tom, and Mary, and little Bess; and, honoured parents, wishing you good health as I am in, thank God, at this present,

"I am your dutiful and loving son,

"JOHN BIRCH.

"P.S. I open my letter to tell you we are going southward immediately, all in high spirits, as there is hopes of meeting the French and Spaniards. We have just hoisted the nun-lady on board an English packet. God send her and this letter safe to England."

Mr. Beaumont might perhaps have been amused by this romantic story, and by the style in which it was told, if he had not been alarmed by the hint at the conclusion of the letter, that the lady was not indifferent to her deliverer. Now Mr. Beaumont earnestly wished that his friend Captain Walsingham might become his brother-in-law; and he began to have fears about this Spanish lady, with her gratitude, her rings, and the advantages of the great interest her misfortunes and helpless condition would excite, together with the vast temptations to fall in love that might occur during the course of a voyage. Had he taken notice of the postscript, his mind would have been somewhat relieved. On this subject Mr. Beaumont pondered all the way that he rode home, and on this subject he was still meditating when he saw his mother standing on the steps, where we left her when Miss Hunter's carriage drove away.

CHAPTER IV

"I shall in all my best obey you, madam."
HAMLET.

"Did you meet Miss Hunter, my dear son?" said she.

"Yes, ma'am, I just passed the carriage in the avenue: she is going home, is not she?" said he, rather in a tone of satisfaction.

"Ah, poor thing! yes," said Mrs. Beaumont, in a most pathetic tone: "ah, poor thing!"

"Why, ma'am, what has happened to her? What's the matter?"

"Matter? Oh, nothing!—Did I say that any thing was the matter? Don't speak so loud," whispered she: "your groom heard every word we said; stay till he is out of hearing, and then we can talk."

"I don't care if all the world hears what I say," cried Mr. Beaumont hastily: but, as if suppressing his rising indignation, he, with a milder look and tone, added, "I cannot conceive, my dear mother, why you are always so afraid of being overheard."

"Servants, my dear, make such mischief, you know, by misunderstanding and misrepresenting every thing they hear; and they repeat things so oddly, and raise such strange reports!"

"True—very true indeed, ma'am," said Mr. Beaumont. "You are quite right, and I beg pardon for being so hasty—I wish you could teach me a little of your patience and prudence."

"Prudence! ah! my dear Edward, 'tis only time and sad experience of the world can teach that to people of our open tempers. I was at your age ten times more imprudent and unsuspicious than you are."

"Were you, ma'am?—But I don't think I am unsuspicious. I was when I was a boy—I wish we could continue children always in some things. I hate suspicion in any body—but more than in any one else, I hate it in myself. And yet—"

Mr. Beaumont hesitated, and his mother instantly went on with a fluent panegyric upon the hereditary unsuspiciousness of his temper.

"But, madam, were you not saying something to me about Miss Hunter?"

"Was I?—Oh, I was merely going to say, that I was sorry you did not know she was going this morning, that you might have taken leave of her, poor thing!"

"Take leave of her! ma'am: I bowed to her, and wished her a good morning, when I met her just now, and she told me she was only going to the hall for a day. Surely no greater leave-taking was requisite, when I am to see the lady again to-morrow, I presume."

"That is not quite so certain as she thinks, poor soul! I told her I would send for her again to-morrow, just to keep up her spirits at leaving me. Walk this way, Edward, under the shade of the trees, for I am dead with the heat; and you, too, look so hot! I say I am not so sure that it would be prudent to have her here so much, especially whilst Mr. Palmer is with us, you know—" Mrs. Beaumont paused, as if waiting for an assent, or a dissent, or a leading hint how to proceed: but her son persisting in perverse silence, she was forced to repeat, "You know, Edward, my dear, you know?"

"I don't know, indeed, ma'am."

"You don't know!"

"Faith, not I, ma'am. I don't know, for the soul of me, what Mr. Palmer's coming has to do with Miss Hunter's going. There's room enough in the house, I suppose, for each of them, and all of us to play our parts. As to the rest, the young lady's coming or going is quite a matter of indifference to me, except, of course, as far as politeness and hospitality go. But all that I leave to you, who do the honours for me so well."

Mrs. Beaumont's ideas were utterly thrown out of their order by this speech, no part of which was exactly what she wished or expected: not that any of the sentiments it contained or suggested were new to her; but she was not prepared to meet them thus clothed in distinct words, and in such a compact form. She had drawn up her forces for battle in an order which this unexpectedly decisive movement of the enemy discomfited; and a less able tactician might have been, in these circumstances, not only embarrassed, but utterly defeated: yet, however unprepared for this sudden shock, with admirable generalship our female Hannibal, falling back in the centre, admitted him to advance impetuous and triumphant, till she had him completely surrounded.

"My being of age in a few days," continued Mr. Beaumont, "will not make any difference, surely; I depend upon it, that you will always invite whomever you like to this house, of which I hope, my dear mother, you will always do me the favour to be the mistress—till I marry, at least. For my wife's feelings," added he, smiling, "I can't engage, before I have her."

"And before we know who she is to be," said Mrs. Beaumont, carelessly. "Time enough, as you say, to think of that. Besides, there are few women in the world, I know scarcely one, with whom, in the relation of mother and daughter-in-law, I should wish to live. But wherever I live, my dear son, as long as I have a house, I hope you will always do me the justice and the pleasure to consider yourself as its master. Heaven knows I shall never give any other man a right to dispute with you the sovereignty of my castle, or my cottage, whichever it may be. As to the rest," pursued Mrs. Beaumont, "you cannot marry against my wishes, my dear Edward; for your wishes on this, as on all other subjects, will ever govern mine."

Her son kissed her hand with warm gratitude.

"You will not, I hope, think that I seek to prolong my regency, or to assume undue power or influence in affairs," continued Mrs. Beaumont, "if I hint to you in general terms what I think may contribute to your happiness. You must afterwards decide for yourself; and are now, as you have ever been, master, to do as you please."

"Too much—too much. I have had too much liberty, and have too little acquired the habit of commanding my will and my passions by my reason. Of this I am sensible. My excellent friend, Captain Walsingham, told me, some years ago, that this was the fault of my character, and he charged me to watch over myself; and so I have; but not so strictly, I fear, as if he had watched along with me.—Well, ma'am, you were going to give me some advice; I am all attention."

"My dear son, Captain Walsingham showed his judgment more, perhaps, in pointing out causes than effects. The weakness of a fond mother, I am sensible, did indulge you in childhood, and, perhaps, more imprudently in youth, with an unlimited liberty to judge and act for yourself. Your mother's system of education came, alas! more from her heart than her head. Captain Walsingham himself cannot be more sensible of my errors than I am."

"Captain Walsingham, believe me, mother, never mentioned this in reproach to you. He is not a man to teach a son to see his mother's errors—if she had any. He always spoke of you with the greatest respect. And since I must, at my own expense, do him justice, it was, I well remember, upon some occasion where I spoke too hastily, and insisted upon my will in opposition to yours, madam, that Captain Walsingham took me aside, and represented to me the fault into which my want of command over myself had betrayed me. This he did so forcibly, that I have never from that hour to this (I flatter myself) on any material occasion, forgotten the impression he made on my mind. But, madam, I interrupt you: you were going to give me your advice about—"

"No, no—no advice—no advice; you are, in my opinion, fully adequate to the direction of your own conduct. I was merely going to suggest, that, since you have not been accustomed to control from a mother, and since you have, thank Heaven! a high spirit, that would sooner break than bend, it must be essential to your happiness to have a wife of a compliant, gentle temper; not fond of disputing the right, or attached to her own opinions; not one who would be tenacious of rule, and unseasonably inflexible."

"Unseasonably inflexible! Undoubtedly, ma'am. Yet I should despise a mean-spirited wife."

"I am sure you would. But compliance that proceeds from affection, you know, can never deserve to be called mean-spirited—nor would it so appear to you. I am persuaded that there is a degree of fondness, of affection, enthusiastic affection, which disposes the temper always to a certain softness and yieldingness, which, I conceive, would be peculiarly attractive to you, and essential to your happiness: in short, I know your temper could not bear contradiction."

"Oh, indeed, ma'am, you are quite mistaken."

"Quite mistaken! and at the very moment he reddens with anger, because I contradict, even in the softest, gentlest manner in my power, his opinion of himself!"

"You don't understand me, indeed, you don't understand me," said Mr. Beaumont, beating with his whip the leaves of a bush which was near him. "Either you don't understand me, or I don't understand you. I am much more able to bear contradiction than you think I am, provided it be direct. But I do not love—what I am doing at this instant," added he, smiling—"I don't love beating about the bush."

"Look there now!—Strange creatures you men are! So like he looks to his poor father, who used to tell me that he loved to be contradicted, and yet who would not, I am sure, have lived three days with any woman who had ventured to contradict him directly. Whatever influence I obtained in his heart, and whatever happiness we enjoyed in our union, I attribute to my trusting to my observations on his character rather than to his own account of himself. Therefore I may be permitted to claim some judgment of what would suit your hereditary temper."

"Certainly, ma'am, certainly. But to come to the point at once, may I ask this plain question—Do you, by these reflections, mean to allude to any particular persons? Is there any woman in the world you at this instant would wish me to marry?"

"Yes—Miss Walsingham."

Mr. Beaumont started with joyful surprise, when his mother thus immediately pronounced the very name he wished to hear.

"You surprise and delight me, my dear mother!"

"Surprise!—How can that be?—Surely you must know my high opinion of Miss Walsingham. But—"

"But—you added but—"

"There is no woman who may not be taxed with a but—yet it is not for her friend to lower her merit. My only objection to her is—I shall infallibly affront you, if I name it."

"Name it! name it! You will not affront me."

"My only objection to her then is, her superiority. She is so superior, that, forgive me, I don't know any man, yourself not excepted, who is at all her equal."

"I think precisely as you do, and rejoice."

"Rejoice? why there I cannot sympathize with you. I own, as a mother, I should feel a little—a little mortified to see my son not the superior; and when the comparison is to be daily and hourly made, and to last for life, and all the world to see it as well as myself. I own I have a mother's vanity. I should wish to see my son always what he has hitherto been—the superior, and master in his own house."

Mr. Beaumont made no reply to these insinuations, but walked on in silence; and his mother, unable to determine precisely whether the vexation apparent in his countenance proceeded from disapprobation of her observations, or from their working the effect she desired upon his pride, warily waited till he should betray some decisive symptom of his feelings. But she waited in vain—he was resolved not to speak.

"There is not a woman upon earth I should wish so much to have as a daughter-in-law, a companion, and a friend, as Miss Walsingham. You must be convinced," resumed Mrs. Beaumont, "so far as I am concerned, it is the most desirable thing in the world. But I should think it my duty to put my own feelings and wishes out of the question, and to make myself prefer whomsoever, all things considered, my judgment tells me would make you the happiest."

"And whom would your judgment prefer, madam?"

"Why—I am not at liberty to tell—unless I could explain all my reasons. Indeed, I know not what to say."

"Dear madam, explain all your reasons, or we shall never understand one another, and never come to an end of these half explanations."

Here they were interrupted by seeing Mr. Twigg, a courtly clergyman, coming towards them. Beaumont was obliged to endure his tiresome flattery upon the beauties of Beaumont Park, and upon the judicious improvements that were making, had been made, and would, no doubt, be very soon made. Mrs. Beaumont, at last, relieved his or her own impatience by commissioning Mr. Twigg to walk round the improvements by himself. By himself she insisted it should be, that she might have his unbiassed judgment upon the two lines which had been marked for the new belt or screen; and he was also to decide whether they should call it a belt or a screen.—Honoured with this commission, he struck off into the walk to which Mrs. Beaumont pointed, and began his solitary progress.

Mr. Beaumont then urged his mother to go on with her explanation. Mrs. Beaumont thought that she could not hazard much by flattering the vanity of a man on that subject on which perhaps it is most easily flattered; therefore, after sufficient delicacy of circumlocution, she informed her son that there was a young lady who was actually dying for love of him; whose extreme fondness would make her live but in him; and who, besides having a natural ductility of character, and softness of temper, was perfectly free from any formidable superiority of intellect, and had the most exalted opinion of his capacity, as well as of his character and accomplishments; in short, such an enthusiastic adoration, as would induce that belief in the infallibility of a husband, which must secure to him the fullest enjoyment of domestic peace, power, and pre-eminence.

Mr. Beaumont seemed less moved than his mother had calculated that the vanity of man must be, by such a declaration—discovery it could not be called. "If I am to take all this seriously, madam," replied he, laughing, "and if, au pied de la lettre my vanity is to believe that this damsel is dying for love; yet, still I have so little chivalry in my nature, that I cannot understand how it would add to my happiness to sacrifice myself to save her life. That I am well suited to her, I am as willing as vanity can make me to believe; but how is it to be proved that the lady is suited to me?"

"My dear, these things do not admit of logical proof."

"Well—moral, sentimental, or any kind of proof you please."

"Have you no pity? and is not pity akin to love?"

"Akin! Oh, yes, ma'am, it is akin; but for that very reason it may not be a friend—relations, you know, in these days, are as often enemies as friends."

"Vile pun! far-fetched quibble!—provoking boy!—But I see you are not in a humour to be serious, so I will take another time to talk to you of this affair."

"Now or never, ma'am, for mercy's sake!"

"Mercy's sake! you who show none—Ah! this is the way with you men; all this is play to you, but death to us."

"Death! dear ma'am; ladies, you know as well as I do, don't die of love in these days—you would not make a fool of your son."

"I could not; nor could any other woman—that is clear: but amongst us, I am afraid we have, undesignedly indeed, but irremediably, made a fool of this poor confiding girl."

"But, ma'am, in whom did she confide? not in me, I'll swear. I have nothing to reproach myself with, thank God!—My conscience is clear; I have been as ungallant as possible. I have been as cruel as my nature would permit. I am sure no one can charge me with giving false promises—I scarcely speak—nor false hopes, for I scarcely look at the young lady."

"So, then, you know who the young lady in question is?"

"Perhaps I ought not to pretend to know."

"That would be useless affectation, alas! for I fear many know, and have seen, and heard, much more than you have—or I either."

Here Mrs. Beaumont observed that her son's colour changed, and that he suddenly grew serious: aware that she had now touched upon the right chord, she struck it again "with a master's hand and prophet's fire." She declared that all the world took it for granted that Miss Hunter was to be married to Mr. Beaumont; that it was talked of every where; that she was asked continually by her correspondents, when the marriage was to take place?—in confirmation of which assertion, she produced bundles of letters from her pockets, from Mrs. and Miss, and from Lady This, and Lady That.

"Nay," continued she, "if it were confined even to the circle of one's private friends and acquaintance, I should not so much mind it, for one might contradict, and have it contradicted, and one might send the poor thing away to some watering-place, and the report might die away, as reports do—sometimes. But all that sort of thing it is too late to think of now—for the thing is public! quite public! got into the newspapers! Here's a paragraph I cut out this very morning from my paper, lest the poor girl should see it. The other day, I believe you saw it yourself, there was something of the same sort. 'We hear that, as soon as he comes of age, Mr. Beaumont, of Beaumont Park, is to lead to the altar of Hymen, Miss Hunter, sister to Sir John Hunter, of Devonshire.' Well,—after you left the room, Albina took up the paper you had been reading; and when she saw this paragraph, I thought she would have dropped. I did not know what to do. Whatever I could say, you know, would only make it worse. I tried to turn it off, and talked of twenty things; but it would not do—no, no, it is too serious for that: well, though I believe she would rather have put her hand in the fire, she had the courage to speak to me about it herself."

"And what did she say, ma'am?" inquired Mr. Beaumont, eagerly.

"Poor simple creature! she had but one idea—that you had seen it! that she would not for the world you had read it. What would you think of her—she should never be able to meet you again—What could she do? It must be contradicted—somebody must contradict it. Then she worried me to have it contradicted in the papers. I told her I did not well know how that could be done, and urged that it would be much more prudent not to fix attention upon the parties by more paragraphs. But she was not in a state to think of prudence;—no. What would you think was the only idea in her mind?—If I would not write, she would write that minute herself, and sign her name. This, and a thousand wild things, she said, till I was forced to be quite angry, and to tell her she must be governed by those who had more discretion than herself. Then she was so subdued, so ashamed—really my heart bled for her, even whilst I scolded her. But it is quite necessary to be harsh with her; for she has no more foresight, nor art, nor command of herself sometimes, than a child of five years old. I assure you, I was rejoiced to get her away before Mr. Palmer came, for a new eye coming into a family sees so much one wouldn't wish to be seen. You know it would be terrible to have the poor young creature commit and expose herself to a stranger so early in life. Indeed, as it is, I am persuaded no one will ever think of marrying her, if you do not.—In worldly prudence—but of that she has not an atom—in worldly prudence she might do better, or as well, certainly; for her fortune will be very considerable. Sir John means to add to it, when he gets the Wigram estate; and the old uncle, Wigram, can't live for ever. But poor Albina, I dare swear, does not know what fortune she is to have, nor what you have. Love! love! all for love!—and all in vain. She is certainly very much to be pitied."

Longer might Mrs. Beaumont have continued in monologue, without danger of interruption from her son, who stood resolved to hear the utmost sum of all that she should say on the subject. Never interrupting her, he only filled certain pauses, that seemed expectant of reply, with the phrases—"I am very sorry, indeed, ma'am"—and, "Really, ma'am, it is out of my power to help it." But Mrs. Beaumont observed that the latter phrase had been omitted as she proceeded—and "I am very sorry indeed, ma'am," he repeated less as words of course, and more and more as if they came from the heart. Having so far, successfully, as she thought, worked upon her son's good-nature, and seeing her daughter through the trees coming towards them, she abruptly exclaimed, "Promise me, at all events, dearest Edward, I conjure you; promise me that you will not make proposals any where else, without letting me know of it beforehand,—and give me time," joining her hands in a supplicating attitude, "give me but a few weeks, to prepare my poor little Albina for this sad, sad stroke!"

"I promise you, madam, that I will not, directly or indirectly, make an offer of my hand or heart to any woman, without previously letting you know my determination. And as for a few weeks, more or less—my mother, surely, need not supplicate, but simply let me know her wishes—even without her reasons, they would have been sufficient with me. Do I satisfy you now, madam?"

"More than satisfy—as you ever do, ever will, my dear son."

"But you will require no more on this subject—I must be left master of myself."

"Indubitably—certainly—master of yourself—most certainly—of course."

Mr. Beaumont was going to add something beginning with, "It is better, at once, to tell you, that I can never—" But Mrs. Beaumont stopped him with, "Hush! my dear, hush! not a word more, for here is Amelia, and I cannot talk on this subject before her, you know.—My beloved Amelia, how languid you look! I fear that, to please me, you have taken too long a walk; and Mr. Palmer won't see you in your best looks, after all.—What note is that you have in your hand?"

"A note from Miss Walsingham, mamma."

"Oh! the chickenpox! take care! letters, notes, every thing may convey the infection," cried Mrs. Beaumont, snatching the paper. "How could dearest Miss Walsingham be so giddy as to answer my note, after what I said in my postscript!—How did this note come?"

"By the little postboy, mamma; I met him at the porter's lodge."

"But what is all this strange thing?" said Mrs. Beaumont, after having read the note twice over.—It contained a certificate from the parish minister and churchwardens, apothecary, and surgeon, bearing witness, one and all, that there was no individual, man, woman, or child, in the parish, or within three miles of Walsingham House, who was even under any suspicion of having the chickenpox.

"My father desires me to send Mrs. Beaumont the enclosed clean bill of health—by which she will find that we need be no longer subject to quarantine; and, unless some other reasons prevent our having the pleasure of seeing her, we may hope soon that she will favour us with her long promised visit.

"Yours, sincerely,

"MARIANNE WALSINGHAM."

"I am delighted," said Mrs. Beaumont, "to find it was a false report, and that we shall not be kept, the Lord knows how long, away from the dear Walsinghams."

"Then we can go to them to-morrow, can't we, mamma? And I will write, and say so, shall I?" said Amelia.

"No need to write, my dear; if we promise for any particular day, and are not able to go, that seems unkind, and is taken ill, you see. And as Mr. Palmer is coming, we can't leave him."

"But he will go with us surely," said Mr. Beaumont. "The Walsinghams are as much his relations as we are; and if he comes two hundred miles to see us, he will, surely, go seven to see them."

"True," said Mrs. Beaumont; "but it is civil and kind to leave him to fix his own day, poor old gentleman. After so long a journey, we must allow him some rest. Consider, he can't go galloping about as you do, dear Edward."

"But," said Amelia, "as the Walsinghams know he is to be in the country, they will of course come to see him immediately."

"How do they know he is to be in the country?"

"I thought—I took it for granted, you told them so, mamma, when you wrote about not going to Walsingham House, on Mr. Walsingham's birthday."

"No, my dear; I was so full of the chickenpox, and terror about you, I could think of nothing else."

"Thank you, dear mother—but now that is out of the question, I had best write a line by the return of the postboy, to say, that Mr. Palmer is to be here to-day, and that he stays only one week."

"Certainly! love—but let me write about it, for I have particular reasons. And, my dear, now we are by ourselves, let me caution you not to mention that Mr. Palmer can stay but one week: in the first place it is uncivil to him, for we are not sure of it, and it is like driving him away; and in the next place, there are reasons I can't explain to you, that know so little of the world, my dear Amelia—but, in general, it is always foolish to mention things."

"Always foolish to mention things!" cried Mr. Beaumont, smiling.

"Of this sort, I mean," said Mrs. Beaumont, a little disconcerted.

"Of what sort?" persisted her son.

"Hush! my dear; here's the postboy and the ass."

"Any letters, my good little boy? Any letters for me?"

"I has, madam, a many for the house. I does not know for who—the bag will tell," said the boy, unstrapping the bag from his shoulders.

"Give it to me, then," said Mrs. Beaumont: "I am anxious for letters always." She was peculiarly anxious now to open the post-bag, to put a stop to a conversation which did not please her. Whilst seated on a rustic seat, under a spreading beech, our heroine, with her accustomed looks of mystery, examined the seals of her numerous and important letters, to ascertain whether they had been opened at the post-office, or whether their folds might have been pervious to any prying eye. Her son tore the covers off the newspapers; and, as he unfolded one, Amelia leaned upon his shoulder, and whispered softly, "Any news of the fleet, brother?"

Mrs. Beaumont, than whom Fine-ear himself had not quicker auditory nerves, especially for indiscreet whispers, looked up from her letters, and examined, unperceived, the countenance of Amelia, who was searching with eagerness the columns of the paper. As Mr. Beaumont turned over the leaf, Amelia looked up, and, seeing her mother's eyes fixed upon her, coloured; and from want of presence of mind to invent any thing better to say, asked if her mother wished to have the papers?

"No," said Mrs. Beaumont, coldly, "not I, Amelia; I am not such a politician as you are grown."

Amelia withdrew her attention, or at least her eyes, from the paper, and had recourse to the beech-tree, the beautiful foliage of which she studied with profound attention.

"God bless me! here's news! news of the fleet!" cried Beaumont, turning suddenly to his sister; and then recollecting himself, to his mother. "Ma'am, they say there has been a great engagement between the French and Spaniards, and the English—particulars not known yet: but, they say, ten sail of the French line are taken, and four Spaniards blown up, and six Spanish men-of-war disabled, and a treasure-ship taken. Walsingham must have been in the engagement—My horse!—I'll gallop over this minute, and know from the Walsinghams if they have seen the papers, and if there's any thing more about it in their papers."

"Gallop! my dearest Edward," said his mother, standing in his path; "but you don't consider Mr. Palmer—"

"Damn Mr. Palmer! I beg your pardon, mother—I mean no harm to the old gentleman—friend of my father's—great respect for him—I'll be back by dinner-time, back ready to receive him—he can't be here till six—only five by me, now! Ma'am, I shall have more than time to dress, too, cool as a cucumber, ready to receive the good old fellow."

"In one short hour, my dear!—seven miles to Walsingham House, and seven back again, and all the time you will waste there, and to dress too—only consider!"

"I do consider, ma'am; and have considered every thing in the world. My horse will carry me there and back in fifty minutes, easily, and five to spare, I'll be bound. I sha'n't light—so where's the paper? I'm off."

"Well—order your horse, and leave me the paper, at least, while he is getting ready. Ride by this way, and you will find us here—where is this famous paragraph?"

Beaumont drew the paper crumpled from the pocket into which he had thrust it—ran off for his horse, and quickly returned mounted. "Give me the paper, good friends!—I'm off."

"Away, then, my dear; since you will heat yourself for nothing. But only let me point out to you," said she, holding the paper fast whilst she held it up to him, "that this whole report rests on no authority whatever; not a word of it in the gazette; not a line from the admiralty; no official account; no bulletin; no credit given to the rumour at Lloyd's; stocks the same.—And how did the news come? Not even the news-writer pretends it came through any the least respectable channel. A frigate in latitude the Lord knows what! saw a fleet in a fog—might be Spanish—might be French—might be English—spoke another frigate some days afterwards, who heard firing: well—firing says nothing. But the frigate turns this firing into an engagement, and a victory; and presently communicates the news to a collier, and the collier tells another collier, and so it goes up the Thames, to some wonder-maker, standing agape for a paragraph, to secure a dinner. To the press the news goes, just as our paper is coming out; and to be sure we shall have a contradiction and an apology in our next."

"Well, ma'am; but I will ask Mr. Walsingham what he thinks, and show him the paper."

"Do, if you like it, my dear; I never control you; but don't overheat yourself for nothing. What can Mr. Walsingham, or all the Walsinghams in the world, tell more than we can? and as to showing him the paper, you know he takes the same paper. But don't let me detain you.—Amelia, who is that coming through the gate? Mr. Palmer's servant, I protest!"

"Well; it can't be, I see!" said Beaumont, dismounting.

"Take away your master's horse—quick—quick!—Amelia, my love, to dress! I must have you ready to receive your godfather's blessing. Consider, Mr. Palmer was your father's earliest friend; and besides, he is a relation, though distant; and it is always a good and prudent thing to keep up relationships. Many a fine estate has come from very distant relations most unexpectedly. And even independently of all relationships, when friendships are properly cultivated, there's no knowing to what they may lead;—not that I look to any thing of that sort here. But before you see Mr. Palmer, just as we are walking home, and quite to ourselves, let me give you some leading hints about this old gentleman's character, which I have gathered, no matter how, for your advantage, my dear children. He is a humourist, and must not be opposed in any of his oddities: he is used to be waited upon, and attended to, as all these men are who have lived in the West Indies. A bon vivant, of course. Edward, produce your best wines—the pilau and currie, and all that, leave to me. I had special notice of his love for a john-doree, and a john-doree I have for him. But now I am going to give you the master-key to his heart. Like all men who have made great fortunes, he loves to feel continually the importance his wealth confers; he loves to feel that wealth does every thing; is superior to every thing—to birth and titles especially: it is his pride to think himself, though a commoner, far above any man who condescends to take a title. He hates persons of quality; therefore, whilst he is here, not a word in favour of any titled person. Forget the whole house of peers—send them all to Coventry—all to Coventry, remember.—And, now you have the key to his heart, go and dress, to be ready for him."

Having thus given her private instructions, and advanced her secret plans, Mrs. Beaumont repaired to her toilet, well satisfied with her morning's work.

CHAPTER V

"Chi mi fa piu carezze che non sole;
O m'ha ingannato, o ingannar me vuole."

"By St. George, there's nothing like Old England for comfort!" cried Mr. Palmer, settling himself in his arm-chair in the evening; "nothing after all in any part of the known world, like Old England for comfort. Why, madam, there's not another people in the universe that have in any of their languages a name even for comfort. The French have been forced to borrow it; but now they have got it, they don't know how to use it, nor even how to pronounce it, poor devils! Well, there's nothing like Old England for comfort."

"Ah! nothing like Old England for comfort!" echoed Mrs. Beaumont, in a sentimental tone, though at that instant her thoughts were far distant from her words; for this declaration of his love for Old England alarmed her with the notion that he might change his mind about returning immediately to Jamaica, and that he might take root again and flourish for years to come in his native soil—perhaps in her neighbourhood, to the bane of all her favourite projects. What would become of her scheme of marrying Amelia to the baronet, and her son to the docile Albina? What would become of the scheme of preventing him from being acquainted with the Walsinghams? For a week it might be practicable to keep them asunder by policising, but this could never be effected if he were to settle, or even to make any long stay, in the country. The Walsinghams would be affronted, and then what would become of their interest in the county? Her son could not be returned without that. And, worse than all the rest, Mr. Palmer might take a fancy to see these Walsinghams, who were as nearly related to him as the Beaumonts; and seeing, he might prefer, and preferring, he might possibly leave half, nay, perhaps the whole, of his large fortune to them,—and thus all her hopes and projects might at once be frustrated. Little aware of the long and perplexing trains of ideas, which his honest ejaculation in favour of his native country had raised, Mr. Palmer went on with his own comfortable thoughts.

"And of all the comforts our native land affords, I know of none so grateful to the heart," continued he, "as good friends, which are to be found nowhere else in such perfection. A man at my time of life misses many an old friend on his return to his native country; but then he sees them still in their representatives, and loves them again in their children. Mr. Beaumont looked at me at that instant, so like his father—he is the image of what my friend was, when I first knew him."

"I am rejoiced you see the likeness," said Mrs. Beaumont. "Amelia, my dear, pour out the coffee."

"And Miss Beaumont, too, has just his expression of countenance, which surprises me more, in her delicate features. Upon my word, I have reason to be proud of my god-daughter, as far as appearances go; and with English women, appearances, fair as they may be, seldom are even so good as the truth. There's her father's smile again for me—young lady, if that smile deceives, there's no truth in woman."

"Do not you find our coffee here very bad, compared with what you have been used to abroad?" said Mrs. Beaumont.

"I do rejoice to find myself here quiet in the country," continued Mr. Palmer, without hearing the lady's question; "nothing after all like a good old English family, where every thing speaks plenty and hospitality, without waste or ostentation; and where you are received with a hearty welcome, without compliments; and let do just as you please, without form, and without being persecuted by politeness."

This was the image of an English country family impressed early upon the good old gentleman's imagination, which had remained there fresh and unchanged since the days of his youth; and he now took it for granted that he should see it realized in the family of his late friend.

"I was afraid," resumed Mrs. Beaumont, "that after being so long accustomed to a West-Indian life, you would find many things unpleasant to your feelings here. But you are so kind, so accommodating. Is it really possible that you have not, since your return to England, experienced any uncomfortable sensations, suffered any serious injury to your health, my dear sir, from the damps and chills of our climate?"

"Why, now I think of it, I have—I have a cough," said Mr. Palmer, coughing.

Mrs. Beaumont officiously shut the window.

"I do acknowledge that England is not quite so superior to all other countries in her climate as in every thing else: yet I don't 'damn the climate like a lord.' At my time of life, a man must expect to be a valetudinarian, and it would be unjust to blame one's native climate for that. But a man of seventy-five must live where he can, not where he will; and Dr. Y— tells me that I can live nowhere but in the West Indies."

"Oh, sir, never mind Dr. Y—," exclaimed young Beaumont: "live with us in England. Many Englishmen live to a great age surely, let people say what they will of the climate."

"But, perhaps, brother," interposed Amelia, "those who, like Mr. Palmer, have lived much in a warm climate, might find a return to a cold country dangerous; and we should consider what is best for him, not merely what is most agreeable to ourselves."

"True, my dearest Amelia," said Mrs. Beaumont; "and to be sure, Dr. Y— is one of our most skilful physicians. I could not be so rash or so selfish as to set my private wishes, or my private opinion, in opposition to Dr. Y—'s advice; but surely, my dear sir, you won't let one physician, however eminent, send you away from us all, and banish you again from England? We have a very clever physician here, Dr. Wheeler, in whom I have the greatest confidence. In my own case, I confess, I should prefer his judgment to any of the London fashionable physicians, who are so fine and so hurried, that they can't take time to study one's particular constitution, and hear all one has to say to them. Now that is Wheeler's great excellence—and I should so like to hear his opinion. I am sure, if he gives it against me, I will not say a word more: if he decide for Jamaica, I may be vexed, but I should make it a point of conscience to submit, and not to urge my good friend to stay in England at his own peril. Happy they who can live where they please, and whose fortune puts it in their power to purchase any climate, and to combine the comforts and luxuries of all countries!"

Nothing more was said upon the subject: Mrs. Beaumont turned the conversation to the different luxuries of the West and East Indies. Mr. Palmer, fatigued by his journey, retired early to rest, little dreaming that his kind hostess waked, whilst he slept, for the purpose of preparing a physician to give a proper opinion upon his case. Mrs. Beaumont left a note to her favourite Dr. Wheeler, to be sent very early in the morning. As if by accident, the doctor dropped in at breakfast time, and Mrs. Beaumont declared that it was the luckiest chance imaginable, that he should happen to call just when she was wishing to see him. When the question in debate was stated to him, he, with becoming gravity of countenance and suavity of manner, entered into a discussion upon the effect of hot and cold climates upon the solids and fluids, and nervous system in general; then upon English constitutions in particular; and, lastly, upon idiosyncrasies.

This last word cost Mr. Palmer half his breakfast: on hearing it he turned down his cup with a profound sigh, and pushed his plate from him; indications which did not escape the physician's demure eye. Gaining confidence from the weakness of the patient, Dr. Wheeler now boldly pronounced, that, in his opinion, any gentleman who, after having habituated himself long to a hot climate, as Jamaica, for instance, should come late in life to reside in a colder climate, as England, for example, must run very great hazard indeed—nay, he could almost venture to predict, would fall a victim to the sudden tension of the lax fibres.

Though a man of sound good sense in most things, Mr. Palmer's weakness was, on medical subjects, as great as his ignorance; his superstitious faith in physicians was as implicit as either Dr. Wheeler or Mrs. Beaumont could desire.

"Then," said Mr. Palmer, with a sigh still deeper than the first—for the first was for himself, and the second for his country—"then England, Old England! farewell for ever! All my judges pronounce sentence of transportation upon me!"

Mr. Beaumont and Amelia, in eager and persuasive tones of remonstrance and expostulation, at once addressed the doctor, to obtain a mitigation or suspension of his sentence. Dr. Wheeler, albeit unused to the imperative mood, reiterated his dictum. Though little accustomed to hold his opinion against the arguments or the wishes of the rich and fair, he, upon this occasion, stood his ground against Miss and Mr. Beaumont wonderfully well for nearly five minutes; till, to his utter perplexity and dismay, he saw Mrs. Beaumont appear amongst his assailants.

"Well, I said I would submit, and not say a word, if Dr. Wheeler was against me," she began; "but I cannot sit by silent: I must protest against this cruel, cruel decree, so contrary too to what I hoped and expected would be Dr. Wheeler's opinion."

Poor Dr. Wheeler twinkled and seemed as if he would have rubbed his eyes, not sure whether he was awake or in a dream. In his perplexity, he apprehended that he had misunderstood Mrs. Beaumont's note, and he now prepared to make his way round again through the solids and the fluids, and the whole nervous system, till, by favour of idiosyncrasy, he hoped to get out of his difficulty, and to allow Mr. Palmer to remain on British ground. Mrs. Beaumont's face, in spite of her powers of simulation, lengthened and lengthened, and darkened and darkened, as he proceeded in his recantation; but, when the exception to the general axiom was fairly made out, and a clear permit to remain in England granted, by such high medical authority, she forced a smile, and joined loudly in the general congratulations. Whilst her son was triumphing and shaking hands with Mr. Palmer, she slipped down stairs after Dr. Wheeler.

"Ah, doctor! What have you done! Ruined me! ruined me! Didn't you read my note? Didn't you understand it?—I thought a word to the wise was enough."

"Why!—then it was as I understood it at first? So I thought; but then I fancied I must be mistaken afterwards; for when I expected support, my dear madam, you opposed my opinion in favour of Jamaica more warmly than any one, and what was I to think?"

"To think! Oh, my dear doctor, you might have guessed that was only a sham opposition."

"But, my dear ma'am," cried Dr. Wheeler, who, though the mildest of men, was now worked up to something like indignation, "my dear ma'am—sham upon sham is too much for any man!"

The doctor went down stairs murmuring. Thus, by excess of hypocrisy, our heroine disgusted even her own adherents, in which she has the honour to resemble some of the most wily politicians famous in English history. But she was too wise ever to let any one who could serve or injure her go discontented out of her presence.

"My dear, good Dr. Wheeler, I never saw you angry before. Come, come," cried Mrs. Beaumont, sliding a douceur into his hand, "friends must not be vexed for trifles; it was only a mistake de part et d'autre, and you'll return here to-morrow, in your way home, and breakfast with us; and now we understand one another. And," added she, in a whisper, "we can talk over things, and have your cool judgment best, when only you, and I, and Mr. Palmer, are present. You comprehend."

Those who practise many manoeuvres, and carry on many intrigues at the same time, have this advantage, that if one fails, the success of another compensates for the disappointment. However she might have been vexed by this slight contre-temps with Dr. Wheeler, Mrs. Beaumont had ample compensation of different sorts this day; some due to her own exertions, some owing to accident. Her own exertions prevented her dear Albina Hunter from returning; for Mrs. Beaumont never sent the promised carriage—only a note of apology—a nail had run into one of the coach-horse's feet. To accident she owed that the Walsinghams were not at home when her son galloped over to see them the next morning, and to inquire what news from Captain Walsingham. That day's paper also brought a contradiction of the report of the engagement and victory; so that Mrs. Beaumont's apprehensions on this subject were allayed; and she had no doubt that, by proper management, with a sufficient number of notes and messages, misunderstandings, lame horses, and crossings upon the road, she might actually get through the week without letting the Walsinghams see Mr. Palmer; or at least without more than a vis, or a morning visit, from which no great danger could be apprehended. "Few, indeed, have so much character," thought she, "or so much dexterity in showing it, as to make a dangerous impression in the course of a formal morning visit."

CHAPTER VI

"Ah! c'est mentir tant soit peu; j'en conviens;
C'est un grand mal—mais il produit un bien."
VOLTAIRE.

The third day went off still more successfully. Dr. Wheeler called at breakfast, frightened Mr. Palmer out of his senses about his health, and convinced him that his life depended upon his immediate return to the climate of Jamaica:—so this point was decided.

Mrs. Beaumont, calculating justly that the Walsinghams would return Mr. Beaumont's visit, and come to pay their respects to Mr. Palmer this morning, settled, as soon as breakfast was over, a plan of operations which should keep Mr. Palmer out till dinner-time. He must see the charming drive which her son had made round his improvements; and she must have the pleasure of showing it to him herself; and she assured him that he might trust to her driving.

So into Mrs. Beaumont's garden-chair he got; and when she had him fairly prisoner, she carried him far away from all danger of intruding visitors. It may readily be supposed that our heroine made good use of the five or six hours' leisure for manoeuvring which she thus secured.

So frank and cordial was this simple-hearted old man, any one but Mrs. Beaumont would have thought that with him no manoeuvring was necessary; that she need only to have trusted to his friendship and generosity, and have directly told him her wishes. He was so prepossessed in her favour, as being the widow of his friend, that he was almost incapable of suspecting her of any unhandsome conduct;

besides, having had little converse with modern ladies, his imagination was so prepossessed with the old-fashioned picture of a respectable widow lady and guardian mother, that he took it for granted Mrs. Beaumont was just like one of the good matrons of former times, like Lady Bountiful, or Lady Lizard; and, as such, he spoke to her of her family concerns, in all the openness of a heart which knew no guile.

"Now, my good Mistress Beaumont, you must look upon me just as my friend the colonel would have done; as a man, who has your family interests at heart just as much as if I were one of yourselves. And let me in to all your little affairs, and trust me with all your little plans, and let us talk over things together, and settle how every thing can be done for the best for the young people. You know, I have no relations in the world but your family and the Walsinghams, of whom, by-the-bye, I know nothing. No one living has any claim upon me: I can leave or give my own just as I please; and you and yours are, of course, my first objects—and for the how, and the what, and the when, I must consult you; and only beg you to keep it in mind, that I would as soon give as bequeath, and rather; for as to what a man leaves to his friends, he can only have the satisfaction of thinking that they will be the better for him after he is dead and gone, which is but cold comfort; but what he gives he has the warm comfort of seeing them enjoy whilst he is alive with them."

"Such a generous sentiment!" exclaimed Mrs. Beaumont, "and so unlike persons in general who have large fortunes at their disposal! I feel so much obliged, so excessively—"

"Not at all, not at all, not at all—no more of that, no more of that, my good lady. The colonel and I were friends; so there can be no obligation between us, nor thanks, nor speeches. But, just as if you were talking to yourself, tell me your mind. And if there are any little embarrassments that the son may want to clear off on coming of age; or if there's any thing wanting to your jointure, my dear madam; or if there should be any marriages in the wind, where a few thousands, more or less, might be the making or the breaking of a heart;—let me hear about it all: and do me the justice to let me have the pleasure of making the young folks, and the old folks too, happy their own way; for I have no notion of insisting on all people being happy my way—no, no! I've too much English liberty in me for that; and I'm sure, you, my good lady, are as great a foe as I am to all family managements and mysteries, where the old don't know what the young do, nor the young what the old think. No, no—that's all nonsense and French convent work—nothing like a good old English family. So, my dear Mistress Beaumont, out with it all, and make me one of yourselves, free of the family from this minute. Here's my hand and heart upon it— an old friend may presume so far."

This frankness would have opened any heart except Mrs. Beaumont's; but it is the misfortune of artful people that they cannot believe others to be artless: either they think simplicity of character folly; or else they suspect that openness is only affected, as a bait to draw them into snares. Our heroine balanced for a moment between these two notions. She could not believe Mr. Palmer to be an absolute fool—no; his having made such a large fortune forbad that thought. Then he must have thrown himself thus open merely to try her, and to come at the knowledge of debts and embarrassments, which, if brought to light, would lower his opinion of the prudence of the family.

"My excellent friend, to be candid with you," she began, "there is no need of your generosity at present, to relieve my son from any embarrassments; for I know that he has no debts whatever. And I am confident he will make my jointure every thing, and more than every thing, I could desire. And, as to marriages, my Amelia is so young, there's time enough to consider."

"True, true; and she does well to take time to consider. But though I don't understand these matters much, she looks mightily like the notion I have of a girl that's a little bit in love."

"In love! Oh, my dear sir! you don't say so—in love?"

"Why, I suppose I should not say in love; there's some other way of expressing it come into fashion since my time, no doubt. And even then, I know that was not to be said of a young lady, till signing and sealing day; but it popped out, and I can't get it back again, so you must even let it pass. And what harm? for you know, madam, without love, what would become of the world?—though I was jilted once and away, I acknowledge—but forgive and forget. I don't like the girl a whit the worse for being a little bit tender-hearted. For I'm morally certain, even from the little I have heard her say, and from the way she has been brought up, and from her being her father's daughter, and her mother's, madam, she could not fix her affections on any one that would not do honour to her choice, or—which is only saying the same thing in other words—that you and I should not approve."

"Ah! there's the thing!" said Mrs. Beaumont, sighing.

"Why now I took it into my head from a blush I saw this morning, though how I came to notice it, I don't know; for to my recollection I have not noticed a girl's blushing before these twenty years—but, to be sure, here I have as near an interest, almost, as if she were my own daughter—I say, from the blush I saw this morning, when young Beaumont was talking of the gallop he had taken to inquire about Captain Walsingham, I took it into my head that he was the happy man."

"Oh! my dear sir, he never made any proposals for Amelia." That was strictly true. "Nor, I am sure, ever thought of it, as far as ever I heard."

The saving clause of "as far as ever I heard," prevented this last assertion from coming under that description of falsehoods denominated downright lies.

"Indeed, how could he?" pursued Mrs. Beaumont, "for you know he is no match for Amelia; he has nothing in the world but his commission. No; there never was any proposal from that quarter; and, of course, it is impossible my daughter could think of a man who has no thoughts of her."

"You know best, my good madam; I merely spoke at random. I'm the worst guesser in the world, especially on these matters: what people tell me, I know; and neither more not less."

Mrs. Beaumont rejoiced in the simplicity of her companion. "Then, my good friend, it is but fair to tell you," said she, "that Amelia has an admirer."

"A lover, hey! Who?"

"Ah, there's the misfortune; it is a thing I never can consent to."

"Ha! then now it is out! There's the reason the girl blushes, and is so absent at times."

A plan now occurred to Mrs. Beaumont's scheming imagination which she thought the master-piece of policy. She determined to account for whatever symptoms of embarrassment Mr. Palmer might observe in her daughter, by attributing them to a thwarted attachment for Sir John Hunter; and Mrs. Beaumont resolved to make a merit to Mr. Palmer of opposing this match because the lover was a baronet, and she thought that Mr. Palmer would be pleased by her showing an aversion to the thoughts of her daughter's marrying a sprig of quality. This ingenious method of paying her court to her open-hearted friend, at the expense equally of truth and of her daughter, she executed with her usual address.

"Well, I'm heartily glad, my dear good madam, to find that you have the same prejudices against sprigs of quality that I have. One good commoner is worth a million of them to my mind. So I told a puppy of a nephew of mine, who would go and buy a baronetage, forsooth—disinherited him! but he is dead, poor puppy."

"Poor young man! But this is all new to me," said Mrs. Beaumont, with well-feigned surprise.

"But did not you know, my dear madam, that I had a nephew, and that he is dead?"

"Oh, yes; but not the particulars."

"No; the particulars I never talk of—not to the poor dog's credit. It's well he's dead, for if he had lived, I am afraid I should have forgiven him. No, no, I never would. But there is no use in thinking any more of that. What were we saying? Oh, about your Amelia—our Amelia, let me call her. If she is so much attached, poor thing, to this man, though he is a baronet, which I own is against him to my fancy, yet it is to be presumed he has good qualities to balance that, since she values him; and young people must be young, and have their little foolish prepossessions for title, and so forth. To be sure, I should have thought my friend's daughter above that, of such a good family as she is, and with such good sense as she inherits too. But we have all our foibles, I suppose. And since it is so with Amelia, why do let me see this baronet-swain of hers, and let me try what good I can find out in him, and let me bring myself, if I can, over my prejudices. And then you, my dear madam, so good and kind a mother as you are, will make an effort too on your part; for we must see the girl happy, if it is not out of all sense and reason. And if the man be worthy of her, it is not his fault that he is a sprig of quality; and we must forgive and forget, and give our consent, my dear Mrs. Beaumont."

"And would you ever give your consent to her marrying Sir John Hunter?" cried Mrs. Beaumont, breathless with amazement, and for a moment thrown off her guard so as to speak quite naturally. The sudden difference in her tone and manner struck even her unsuspicious companion, and he attributed it to displeasure at this last hint.

"Why, my very dear good friend's wife, forgive me," said he, "for this interference, and for, as it seems, opposing your opinion about your daughter's marriage, which no man has a right to do—but if you ask me plump whether I could forgive her for marrying Sir John Hunter, I answer, for I can speak nothing but the truth, I would, if he is a worthy man."

"I thought," said Mrs. Beaumont, astonished, "you disinherited your own nephew, because he took a baronet's title against your will."

"Bless you! no, my dear madam—that did displease me, to be sure—but that was the least cause of displeasure I had. I let the world fancy and say what they would, rather than bring faults to light.—But no more about that."

"But did not you take an oath that you would never leave a shilling of your fortune to any sprig of quality?"

"Never! my dearest madam! never," cried Mr. Palmer, laughing. "Never was such a gander. See what oaths people put into one's mouth."

"And what lies the world tells," said Mrs. Beaumont.

"And believes," said Mr. Palmer, with a sly smile.

The surprise that Mrs. Beaumont felt was mixed with a strange and rapid confusion of other sentiments, regret for having wasted such a quantity of contrivance and manoeuvring against an imaginary difficulty. All this arose from her too easy belief of secret underhand information.

Through the maze of artifice in which she had involved affairs, she now, with some difficulty, perceived that plain truth would have served her purpose better. But regret for the past was not in the least mixed with any thing like remorse or penitence; on the contrary, she instantly began to consider how she could best profit by her own wrong. She thought she saw two of her favourite objects almost within her reach, Mr. Palmer's fortune, and the future title for her daughter: no obstacle seemed likely to oppose the accomplishment of her wishes, except Amelia's own inclinations: these she thought she could readily prevail upon her to give up; for she knew that her daughter was both of a timid and of an affectionate temper; that she had never in any instance withstood, or even disputed, her maternal authority; and that dread of her displeasure had often proved sufficient to make Amelia suppress or sacrifice her own feelings. Combining all these reflections with her wonted rapidity, Mrs. Beaumont determined what her play should now be. She saw, or thought she saw, that she ought, either by gentle or strong means, to lure or intimidate Amelia to her purpose; and that, while she carried on this part of the plot with her daughter in private, she should appear to Mr. Palmer to yield to his persuasions by degrees, to make the young people happy their own way, and to be persuaded reluctantly out of her aversion to sprigs of quality. To be sure, it would be necessary to give fresh explanations and instructions to Sir John Hunter, through his sister, with the new parts that he and she were to act in this domestic drama. As soon as Mrs. Beaumont returned from her airing, therefore, she retired to her own apartment, and wrote a note of explanation, with a proper proportion of sentiment and verbiage, to her dear Albina, begging to see her and Sir John Hunter the very next day. The horse, which had been lamed by the nail, now, of course, had recovered; and it was found by Mrs. Beaumont that she had been misinformed, and that he had been lamed only by sudden cramp. Any excuse she knew would be sufficient, in the present state of affairs, to the young lady, who was more ready to be deceived than even our heroine was disposed to deceive. Indeed, as Machiavel says, "as there are people willing to cheat, there will always be those who are ready to be cheated."

CHAPTER VII

"Vous m'enchantez, mais vous m'épouvantez;
Ces pieges-là sont-ils bien ajustés?
Craignez vous point de vous laisser surprendre
Dans les filets que vos mains savent tendre?"
VOLTAIRE.

To prepare Amelia to receive Sir John Hunter properly was Mrs. Beaumont's next attempt; for as she had represented to Mr. Palmer that her daughter was attached to Sir John, it was necessary that her manner should in some degree accord with this representation, that at least it should not exhibit any symptoms of disapprobation or dislike: whatever coldness or reserve might appear, it would be easy to attribute to bashfulness and dread of Mr. Palmer's observation. When Amelia was undressing at night, her mother went into her room; and, having dismissed the maid, threw herself into an arm-chair, and exclaimed, half-yawning, "How tired I am!—No wonder, such a long airing as we took to-day. But, my dear Amelia, I could not sleep to-night without telling you how glad I am to find that you are such a favourite with Mr. Palmer."

"I am glad he likes me," said Amelia; "I am sure I like him. What a benevolent, excellent man he seems to be!"

"Excellent, excellent—the best creature in the world!—And so interested about you! and so anxious that you should be well and soon established; almost as anxious about it as I am myself."

"He is very good—and you are very good, mamma; but there is no occasion that I should be soon established, as it is called—is there?"

"That is the regular answer, you know, in these cases, from every young lady that ever was born, in or out of a book within the memory of man. But we will suppose all that to be said prettily on your part, and answered properly on mine: so give me leave to go on to something more to the purpose; and don't look so alarmed, my love. You know, I am not a hurrying person; you shall take your own time, and every thing shall be done as you like, and the whole shall be kept amongst ourselves entirely; for nothing is so disadvantageous and distressing to a young woman as to have these things talked of in the world long before they take place."

"But, ma'am!—Surely there is no marriage determined upon for me, without my even knowing it."

"Determined upon!—Oh dear, no, my darling. You shall decide every thing for yourself."

"Thank you, mother; now you are kind indeed."

"Indubitably, my dearest Amelia, I would not decide on any thing without consulting you: for I have the greatest dependence on your prudence and judgment. With a silly romantic girl, who had no discretion, I should certainly think it my duty to do otherwise; and if I saw my daughter following headlong some idle fancy of fifteen, I should interpose my authority at once, and say, It must not be. But I know my Amelia so well, that I am confident she will judge as prudently for herself as I could for her; and indeed, I am persuaded that our opinions will be now, as they almost always are, my sweet girl, the same."

"I hope so mamma—but—"

"Well, well, I'll allow a maidenly but—and you will allow that Sir John Hunter shall be the man at last."

"Oh, mamma, that can never be," said Amelia, with much earnestness.

"Never—A young lady's never, Amelia, I will allow too. Don't interrupt me, my dear—but give me leave to tell you again, that you shall have your own time—Mr. Palmer has given his consent and approbation."

"Consent and approbation!" cried Amelia. "And is it come to this? without even consulting me! And is this the way I am left to judge for myself?—Oh, mother! mother! what will become of me?"

Amelia, who had long had experience that it was vain for her to attempt to counteract or oppose any scheme that her mother had planned, sat down at this instant in despair: but even from despair she took courage; and, rising suddenly, exclaimed, "I never can or will marry Sir John Hunter—for I love another person—mother, you know I do—and I will speak truth, and abide by it, let the consequences be what they may."

"Well, my dear, don't speak so loud, at all events; for though it may be very proper to speak the truth, it is not necessary that the whole universe should hear it. You speak of another attachment—is it possible that you allude to Captain Walsingham? But Captain Walsingham has never proposed for you, nor even given you any reason to think he would; or if he has, he must have deceived me in the grossest manner."

"He is incapable of deceiving any body," said Amelia. "He never gave me any reason to think he would propose for me; nor ever made the slightest attempt to engage my affections. You saw his conduct: it was always uniform. He is incapable of any double or underhand practices."

"In the warmth of your eulogium on Captain Walsingham, you seem, Amelia, to forget that you reflect, in the most severe manner, upon yourself: for what woman, what young woman especially, who has either delicacy, pride, or prudence, can avow that she loves a man, who has never given, even by her own statement of the matter, the slightest reason to believe that he thinks of her?"

Amelia stood abashed, and for some instants incapable of reply: but at last, approaching her mother, and hiding her face, as she hung over her shoulder, she said, in a low and timid voice, "It was only to my mother—I thought that could not be wrong—and when it was to prevent a greater wrong, the engaging myself to another person."

"Engaging yourself, my foolish child! but did I not tell you that you should have your own time?"

"But no time, mother, will do."

"Try, my dear love; that is all I ask of you; and this you cannot, in duty, in kindness, in prudence, or with decency, refuse me."

"Cannot I?"

"Indeed you cannot. So say not a word more that can lessen the high opinion I have of you; but show me that you have a becoming sense of your own and of female dignity, and that you are not the poor, mean-spirited creature, to pine for a man who disdains you."

"Disdain! I never saw any disdain. On the contrary, though he never gave me reason to think so, I cannot help fancying—"

"That he likes you—and yet he never proposed for you! Do not believe it—a man may coquet as well as a woman, and often more; but till he makes his proposal, never, if you have any value for your own happiness or dignity, fancy for a moment that he loves you."

"But he cannot marry, because he is so poor."

"True—and if so, what stronger argument can be brought against your thinking of him?"

"I do not think of him—I endeavour not to think of him."

"That is my own girl! Depend upon it, he thinks not of you. He is all in his profession—prefers it to every woman upon earth. I have heard him say he would not give it up for any consideration. All for glory, you see; nothing for love."

Amelia sighed. Her mother rose, and kissing her, said, as if she took every thing she wished for granted, "So, my Amelia, I am glad to see you reasonable, and ready to show a spirit that becomes you—Sir John Hunter breakfasts here to-morrow."

"But," said Amelia, detaining her mother, who would have left the room, "I cannot encourage Sir John Hunter, for I do not esteem him; therefore I am sure I can never love him."

"You cannot encourage Sir John Hunter, Amelia?" replied Mrs. Beaumont. "It is extraordinary that this should appear to you an impossibility the very moment the gentleman proposes for you. It was not always so. Allow me to remind you of a ball last year, where you and I met both Sir John Hunter and Captain Walsingham; as I remember, you gave all your attention that evening to Sir John."

"Oh, mother, I am ashamed of that evening—I regret it more than any evening of my life. I did wrong, very wrong; and bitterly have I suffered for it, as people always do, sooner or later, by deceit. I was afraid that you should see my real feelings; and, to conceal them, I, for the first and last time of my life, acted like a coquette. But if you recollect, dear mother, the very next day I confessed the truth to you. My friend, Miss Walsingham, urged me to have the courage to be sincere."

"Miss Walsingham! On every occasion I find the secret influence of these Walsinghams operating in my family," cried Mrs. Beaumont, from a sudden impulse of anger, which threw her off her guard.

"Surely their influence has always been beneficial to us all. To me, Miss Walsingham's friendship has been of the greatest service."

"Yes; by secretly encouraging you, against your mother's approbation, in a ridiculous passion for a man who neither can nor will marry you."

"Far from encouraging me, madam, in any thing contrary to your wishes—and far from wishing to do any thing secretly, Miss Walsingham never spoke to me on this subject but once; and that was to advise me strongly not to conceal the truth from you, and not to make use of any artifices or manoeuvres."

"Possibly, very possibly; but I presume you could conduct yourself properly without Miss Walsingham's interference or advice."

"I thought, mamma, you liked Miss Walsingham particularly, and that you wished I should cultivate her friendship."

"Certainly; I admire Miss Walsingham extremely, and wish to be on the best terms with the family; but I will never permit any one to interfere between me and my children. We should have gone on better without advisers."

"I am sure her advice and friendship have preserved me from many faults, but never led me into any. I might, from timidity, and from fear of your superior address and abilities, have become insincere and artful; but she has given me strength of mind enough to bear the present evil, and to dare at all hazards to speak the truth."

"But, my dearest Amelia," said Mrs. Beaumont, softening her tone, "why so warm? What object can your mother have but your good? Can any Miss Walsingham, or any other friend upon earth, have your interest so much at heart as I have? Why am I so anxious, if it is not from love to you?"

Amelia was touched by her mother's looks and words of affection, and acknowledged that she had spoken with too much warmth.

Mrs. Beaumont thought she could make advantage of this moment.

"Then, my beloved child, if you are convinced of my affection for you, show at least some confidence in me in return: show some disposition to oblige me. Here is a match I approve; here is an establishment every way suitable."

"But why, mamma, must I be married?" interrupted Amelia. "I will not think, at least I will try not to think, of any one of whom you do not approve; but I cannot marry any other man while I feel such a partiality for—. So, dear mother, pray do not let Sir John Hunter come here any more on my account. It is not necessary that I should marry."

"It is necessary, however," said Mrs. Beaumont, withdrawing her hand haughtily, and darting a look of contempt and anger upon her daughter, "it is necessary, however, that I should be mistress in my own house, and that I should invite here whomever I please. And it is necessary that you should receive them without airs, and with politeness. On this, observe, I insist, and will be obeyed."

Mrs. Beaumont would receive no reply, but left the room seemingly in great displeasure: but even half her anger was affected, to intimidate this gentle girl.

Sir John Hunter and his sister arrived to breakfast. Mrs. Beaumont played her part admirably; so that she seemed to Mr. Palmer only to be enduring Sir John from consideration for her daughter, and from compliance with Mr. Palmer's own request that she would try what could be done to make the young people happy; yet she, with infinite address, drew Sir John out, and dexterously turned every thing he said into what she thought would please Mr. Palmer, though all the time she seemed to be misunderstanding or confuting him. Mr. Palmer's attention, which was generally fixed exclusively on one object at a time, had ample occupation in studying Sir John, whom he examined, for Amelia's sake, with all the honest penetration which he possessed. Towards Amelia herself he scarcely ever looked; for, without any refinement of delicacy, he had sufficient feeling and sense to avoid what he thought would embarrass a young lady. Amelia's silence and reserve appeared to him, therefore, as her politic mother had foreseen, just what was natural and proper. He had been told that she was attached to Sir John Hunter; and the idea of doubting the truth of what Mrs. Beaumont had asserted could not enter his confiding mind.

In the mean time, our heroine, to whom the conduct of a double intrigue was by no means embarrassing, did not neglect the affairs of her dear Albina: she had found time before breakfast, as she met Miss Hunter getting out of her carriage, to make herself sure that her notes of explanation had been understood; and she now, by a multitude of scarcely perceptible inuendoes, and seemingly suppressed looks of pity, contrived to carry on the representation she had made to her son of this damsel's helpless and lovelorn state. Indeed, the young lady appeared as much in love as could have been desired for stage effect, and rather more than was necessary for propriety. All Mrs. Beaumont's art, therefore, was exerted to throw a veil of becoming delicacy over what might have been too glaring, by hiding half to improve the whole. Where there was any want of management on the part of her young coadjutrix, she, with exquisite skill, made advantage even of these errors by look? and sighs, that implied almost as emphatically as words could have said to her son—"You see what I told you is too true. The simple creature has not art enough to conceal her passion. She is undone in the eyes of the world, if you do not confirm what report has said."

This she left to work its natural effect upon the vanity of man. And in the midst of these multiplied manoeuvres, Mrs. Beaumont sat with ease and unconcern, sometimes talking to one, sometimes to another; so that a stranger would have thought her a party uninterested in all that was going forward, and might have wondered at her blindness or indifference.

But, alas! notwithstanding her utmost art, she failed this day in turning and twisting Sir John Hunter's conversation and character so as to make them agreeable to Mr. Palmer. This she knew by his retiring at an early hour at night, as he sometimes did when company was not agreeable to him. His age gave him this privilege. Mrs. Beaumont followed, to inquire if he would not wish to take something before he went to rest.

"By St. George, Madam Beaumont, you are right," said Mr. Palmer, "you are right, in not liking this baronet. I'm tired of him—sick of him—can't like him!—sorry for it, since Amelia likes him. But what can a daughter of Colonel Beaumont find in this man to be pleased with? He is a baronet, to be sure, but that is all. Tell me, my good madam, what it is the girl likes in him?"

Mrs. Beaumont could only answer by an equivocal smile, and a shrug, that seemed to say—there's no accounting for these things.

"But, my dear madam," pursued Mr. Palmer, "the man is neither handsome nor young: he is old enough for her father, though he gives himself the airs of a youngster; and his manners are—I can allow for fashionable manners. But, madam, it is his character I don't like—selfish—cold—designing—not a generous thought, not a good feeling about him. You are right, madam, quite right. In all his conversation such meanness, and even in what he means for wit, such a contempt of what is fair and honourable! Now that fellow does not believe that such a thing as virtue or patriotism, honour or friendship, exists. The jackanapes!—and as for love! why, madam, I'm convinced he is no more in love with the girl than I am, nor so much, ma'am, nor half so much!—does not feel her merit, does not value her accomplishments, does not Madam! madam! he is thinking of nothing but himself, and her fortune—fortune! fortune! fortune! that's all. The man's a miser. Madam, they that know no better fancy that there are none but old misers; but I can tell them there are young misers, and middle-aged misers, and misers of all ages. They say such a man can't be a miser, because he is a spendthrift; but, madam, you know a man can be both—yes, and that's what many of your young men of fashion are, and what, I'll engage, this fellow is. And can Amelia like him? my poor child! and does she think he loves her? my poor, poor child! how can she be so blind? but love is always blind, they say. I've a great mind to take her to task, and ask her, between ourselves, what it is she likes in her baronet."

"Oh, my dear sir! she would sink to the centre of the earth if you were to speak. For Heaven's sake, don't take her to task, foolish as she is; besides, she would be so angry with me for telling you."

"Angry? the gipsy! Am not I her godfather and her guardian? though I could not act, because I was abroad, yet her guardian I was left by her father, and love her too as well as I should a daughter of her father's—and she to have secrets, and mysteries! that would be worse than all the rest, for mysteries are what I abhor. Madam, wherever there are secrets and mysteries in a family, take my word for it, there is somethings wrong."

"True, my dear sir; but Amelia has no idea of mysteries or art. I only meant that young girls, you know, will be ashamed on these occasions, and we must make allowances. So do not speak to her, I conjure you."

"Well, madam, you are her mother, and must know best. I have only her interest at heart: but I won't speak to her, since it will so distress her. But what shall be done about this lover? You are quite right about him, and I have not a word more to say."

"But I declare I think you judge him too harshly. Though I am not inclined to be his friend, yet I must do him the justice to say, he has more good qualities than you allow, or rather than you have seen yet. He is passionately fond of Amelia. Oh, there you're wrong, quite wrong; he is passionately in love, whatever he may pretend to the contrary."

"Pretend! and why should the puppy pretend not to be in love?"

"Pride, pride and fashion. Young men are so governed by fashion, and so afraid of ridicule. There's a set of fashionables now, with whom love is a bore, you know."

"I know! no, indeed, I know no such thing," said Mr. Palmer. "But this I know, that I hate pretences of all sorts; and if the man is in love, I should, for my part, like him the better for showing it."

"So he will, when you know him a little better. You are quite a stranger, and he is bashful."

"Bashful! Never saw so confident a man in any country."

"But he is shy under all that."

"Under! But I don't like characters where every thing is under something different from what appears at top."

"Well, take a day or two more to study him. Though I am his enemy, I must deal fairly by him, for poor Amelia's sake."

"You are a good mother, madam, an indulgent mother, and I honour and love you for it. I'll follow your example, and bear with this spendthrift-miser-coxcomb sprig of quality for a day or two more, and try to like him, for Amelia's sake. But, if he's not worthy of her, he sha'n't have her, by St. George, he shall not—shall he, madam?"

"Oh, no, no; good night, my good sir."

What the manoeuvres of the next day might have effected, and how far Sir John Hunter profited by the new instructions which were given to him in consequence of this conversation, can never be accurately ascertained, because the whole united plan of operations was disturbed by a new and unforeseen event.

CHAPTER VIII

"Un volto senza senno,
Un petto senza core, un cor senz' alma,
Un' alma senza fede."
GUARINI.

"Here's glorious news of Captain Walsingham!" cried young Beaumont; "I always knew he would distinguish himself if he had an opportunity; and, thank God! he has had as fine an opportunity as heart could wish. Here, mother! here, Mr. Palmer, is an account of it in this day's paper! and here is a letter from himself, which Mr. Walsingham has just sent me."

"Oh, give me the letter," cried Mrs. Beaumont, with affected eagerness.

"Let me have the paper, then," cried Mr. Palmer. "Where are my spectacles?"

"Are there any letters for me?" said Sir John Hunter. "Did my newspapers come? Albina, I desired that they should be forwarded here. Mrs. Beaumont, can you tell me any thing of my papers?"

"Dear Amelia, how interesting your brother looks when he is pleased!" Albina whispered, quite loud enough to be heard.

"A most gallant action, by St. George!" exclaimed Mr. Palmer. "These are the things that keep up the honour of the British navy, and the glory of Britain."

"This Spanish ship that Captain Walsingham captured the day after the engagement is likely to turn out a valuable prize, too," said Mrs. Beaumont. "I am vastly glad to find this by his letter, for the money will be useful to him, he wanted it so much. He does not say how much his share will come to, does he, Edward?"

"No, ma'am: you see he writes in a great hurry, and he has only time, as he says, to mention the needful."

"And is not the money the needful?" said Sir John Hunter, with a splenetic smile.

"With Walsingham it is only a secondary consideration," replied Beaumont; "honour is Captain Walsingham's first object. I dare say he has never yet calculated what his prize-money will be."

"Right, right!" reiterated Mr. Palmer; "then he is the right sort. Long may it be before our naval officers think more of prize-money than of glory! Long may it be before our honest tars turn into calculating pirates!"

"They never will or can whilst they have such officers as Captain Walsingham," said Beaumont.

"By St. George, he seems to be a fine fellow, and you a warm friend," said Mr. Palmer. "Ay, ay, the colonel's own son. But why have I never seen any of these Walsinghams since I came to the country? Are they ashamed of being related to me, because I am a merchant?"

"More likely they are too proud to pay court to you because you are so rich," said Mr. Beaumont. "But they did come to see you, sir,—the morning you were out so late, mother, you know."

"Oh, ay, true—how unfortunate!"

"But have not we horses? have not we carriages? have not we legs?" said Mr. Palmer. "I'll go and see these Walsinghams to-morrow, please God I live so long: for I am proud of my relationship to this young hero; and I won't be cast off by good people, let them be as proud as they will—that's their fault—but I will not stand on idle ceremony: so, my good Mistress Beaumont, we will all go in a body, and storm their castle to-morrow morning."

"An admirable plan! I like it of all things!" said Mrs. Beaumont. "How few, even in youth, are so active and enthusiastic as our good friend! But, my dear Mr. Palmer—"

"But I wish I could see the captain himself. Is there any chance of his coming home?"

"Home! yes," said Beaumont: "did you not read his letter, sir? here it is; he will be at home directly. He says, 'perhaps a few hours after this letter reaches you, you'll see me.'"

"See him! Odds my life, I'm glad of it. And you, my little Amelia," said Mr. Palmer, tapping her shoulders as she stood with her back to him reading the newspaper; "and you, my little silent one, not one word have I heard from you all this time. Does not some spark of your father's spirit kindle within you on hearing of this heroic relation of ours?"

"Luckily for the ladies, sir," said Sir John Hunter, coming up, as he thought, to the lady's assistance— "luckily for young ladies, sir, they are not called upon to be heroes; and it would be luckier still for us men, if they never set themselves up for heroines—Ha! ha! ha! Miss Beaumont," continued he, "the shower is over; I'll order the horses out, that we may have our ride." Sir John left the room, evidently pleased with his own wit.

"Amelia, my love," said Mrs. Beaumont, who drew up also to give assistance at this critical juncture, "go, this moment, and write a note to your friend Miss Walsingham, to say that we shall all be with them early to-morrow: I will send a servant directly, that we may be sure to meet with them at home this time; you'll find pen, ink, and paper in my dressing-room, love."

Mrs. Beaumont drew Amelia's arm within hers, and, dictating kindest messages for the Walsinghams, led her out of the room. Having thus successfully covered her daughter's retreat, our skilful manoeuvrer returned, all self-complacent, to the company. And next, to please the warm-hearted Mr. Palmer, she seemed to sympathize in his patriotic enthusiasm for the British navy: she pronounced a panegyric on the young hero, Captain Walsingham, which made the good old man rub his hands with exultation, and which irradiated with joy the countenance of her son. But, alas! Mrs. Beaumont's endeavours to please, or rather to dupe all parties, could not, even with her consummate address, always succeed: though she had an excellent memory, and great presence of mind, with peculiar quickness both of eye and ear, yet she could not always register, arrange, and recollect all that was necessary for the various parts she undertook to act. Scarcely had she finished her eulogium on Captain Walsingham, when, to her dismay, she saw close behind her Sir John Hunter, who had entered the room without her perceiving it. He said not one word; but his clouded brow showed his suspicions, and his extreme displeasure.

"Mrs. Beaumont," said he, after some minutes' silence, "I find I must have the honour of wishing you a good morning, for I have an indispensable engagement at home to dinner to-day."

"I thought, Sir John, you and Amelia were going to ride?"

"Ma'am, Miss Beaumont does not choose to ride—she told me, so this instant as I passed her on the stairs. Oh! don't disturb her, I beg—she is writing to Miss Walsingham—I have the honour to wish you a good morning, ma'am."

"Well, if you are determined to go, let me say three words to you in the music-room, Sir John: though," added she, in a whisper intended to be heard by Mr. Palmer, "I know you do not look upon me as your friend, yet depend upon it I shall treat you and all the world with perfect candour."

Sir John, though sulky, could not avoid following the lady; and as soon as she had shut all the doors and double-doors of the music-room, she exclaimed, "It is always best to speak openly to one's friends. Now, my dear Sir John Hunter, how can you be so childish as to take ill of me what I really was forced to say, for your interest, about Captain Walsingham, to Mr. Palmer? You know old Palmer is the oddest, most self-willed man imaginable! humour and please him I must, the few days he is with me. You know he goes on Tuesday—that's decided—Dr. Wheeler has seen him, has talked to him about his health, and it is absolutely necessary that he should return to the West Indies. Then he is perfectly determined to leave all he has to Amelia."

"Yes, ma'am; but how am I sure of being the better for that?" interrupted Sir John, whose decided selfishness was a match for Mrs. Beaumont's address, because it went without scruple or ceremony straight to his object; "for, ma'am, you can't think I'm such a fool as not to see that Mr. Palmer wishes me at the devil. Miss Beaumont gives me no encouragement; and you, ma'am, I know, are too good a politician to offend Mr. Palmer: so, if he declares in favour of this young hero, Captain Walsingham, I may quit the field."

"But you don't consider that Mr. Palmer's young hero has never made any proposal for Amelia."

"Pshaw! ma'am—but I know, as well as you do, that he likes her, and propose he will for her now that he has money."

"Granting that; you forget that all this takes time, and that Palmer will be gone to the West Indies before they can bring out their proposal; and as soon as he is gone, and has left his will, as he means to do, with me, you and I have the game in our own hands. It is very extraordinary to me that you do not seem to understand my play, though I explained the whole to Albina; and I thought she had made you comprehend the necessity for my seeming, for this one week, to be less your friend than I could wish, because of your title, and that odd whim of Palmer, you know: but I am sure we understand one another now."

"Excuse me," said the invincible Sir John: "I confess, Mrs. Beaumont, you have so much more abilities, and finesse, and all that sort of thing, than I have, that I cannot help being afraid of—of not understanding the business rightly. In business there is nothing like understanding one another, and going on sure grounds. There has been so much going backwards and forwards, and explanations and manoeuvres, that I am not clear how it is; nor do I feel secure even that I have the honour of your approbation."

"What! not when I have assured you of it, Sir John, in the most unequivocal manner?"

It was singular that the only person to whom in this affair Mrs. Beaumont spoke the real truth should not believe her. Sir John Hunter continued obstinately suspicious and incredulous. He had just heard that his uncle Wigram, his rich uncle Wigram, was taken ill, and not likely to recover. This intelligence had also reached Mrs. Beaumont, and she was anxious to secure the baronet and the Wigram fortune for her daughter; but nothing she could say seemed to satisfy him that she was not double-dealing. At last, to prove to him her sincerity, she gave him what he required, and what alone, he said, could make his mind easy, could bring him to make up his mind—a written assurance of her approbation of his addresses to Amelia. With this he was content; "for," said he, "what is written remains, and there can be no misunderstandings in future, or changing of minds."

It was agreed between these confidential friends, that Sir John should depart, as it were, displeased; and she begged that he would not return till Mr. Palmer should have left the country.

Now there was a numerous tribe of hangers-on, who were in the habit of frequenting Beaumont Park, whom Mrs. Beaumont loved to see at her house; because, besides making her feel her own importance, they were frequently useful to carry on the subordinate parts of her perpetual manoeuvres. Among these secondary personages who attended Mrs. Beaumont abroad to increase her consequence in the eyes of common spectators, and who at home filled the stage, and added to the bustle and effect, her chief favourites were Mr. Twigg (the same gentleman who was deputed to decide upon the belt or the screen) and Captain Lightbody. Mr. Twigg was the most, elegant flatterer of the two, but Captain Lightbody was the most assured, and upon the whole made his way the best. He was a handsome man, had a good address, could tell a good story, sing a good song, and make things go off well, when there was company; so that he was a prodigious assistance to the mistress of the house. Then he danced with the young ladies when they had no other partners; he mounted guard regularly beside the piano-forte, or the harp, when the ladies were playing; and at dinner it was always the etiquette for him to sit beside Miss Beaumont, or Miss Hunter, when the gentlemen guests were not such as Mrs. Beaumont thought entitled to that honour, or such as she deemed safe companions. These arrangements imply that Captain Lightbody thought himself in Mrs. Beaumont's confidence: and so he was to a certain degree, just enough to flatter him into doing her high or low behests. Whenever she had a report to circulate, or to contradict, Captain Lightbody was put in play; and no man could be better calculated for this purpose, both from his love of talking, and of locomotion. He galloped about from place to place, and from one great house to another; knew all the lords and ladies, and generals and colonels, and brigade-majors and aides-de-camp, in the land. Could any mortal be better qualified to fetch and carry news for Mrs. Beaumont? Besides news, it was his office to carry compliments, and to speed the intercourse, not perhaps from soul to soul, but from house to house, which is necessary in a visiting country to keep up the character of an agreeable neighbour. Did Mrs. Beaumont forget to send a card of invitation, or neglect to return a visit, Lightbody was to set it to rights for her, Lightbody, the ready bearer of pretty notes, the maker always, the fabricator sometimes, of the civilest speeches imaginable. This expert speechifier, this ever idle, ever busy scamperer, our heroine dispatched to engage a neighbouring family to pay her a morning visit the next day, just about the time which was fixed for her going to see the Walsinghams. The usual caution was given. "Pray, Lightbody, do not let my name be used; do not let me be mentioned; but take it upon yourself, and say, as if from yourself, that you have reason to believe I take it ill that they have not been here lately. And then you can mention the hour that would be most convenient. But let me have nothing to do with it. I must not appear in it on any account."

In consequence of Captain Lightbody's faithful execution of his secret instructions, a barouche full of morning visitors drove to the door, just at the time when Mrs. Beaumont had proposed to set out for Walsingham House. Mrs. Beaumont, with a well-dissembled look of vexation, exclaimed, as she looked out of the window at the carriage, "How provoking! Who can these people be? I hope Martin will say I am not at home. Ring—ring, Amelia. Oh, it's too late, they have seen me! and Martin, stupid creature! has let them in."

Mr. Palmer was much discomfited, and grew more and more impatient when these troublesome visitors protracted their stay, and proposed a walk to see some improvements in the grounds.

"But, my good Mistress Beaumont," said he, "you know we are engaged to our cousin Walsingham this morning; and if you will give me leave, I will go on before you with Mr. Beaumont, and we can say what detains you."

Disconcerted by this simple determination of this straight-forward, plain-spoken old gentleman, Mrs. Beaumont saw that farther delay on her part would be not only inefficacious, but dangerous. She now was eager to be relieved from the difficulties which she had herself contrived. She would not, for any consideration, have trusted Mr. Palmer to pay this visit without her: therefore, by an able counter-movement, she extricated herself not only without loss, but with advantage, from this perilous situation. She made a handsome apology to her visitors for being obliged to run away from them. "She would leave Amelia to have the pleasure of showing them the grounds."

Mrs. Beaumont was irresistible in her arrangements. Amelia, disappointed and afraid to show how deeply she felt the disappointment, was obliged to stay to do the honours of Beaumont Park, whilst her mother drove off rejoicing in half the success, at least, of her stratagem; but even as a politician she used upon every occasion too much artifice. It was said of Cardinal Mazarin, he is a great politician, but in all his politics there is one capital defect—"C'est qu'il veut toujours tromper."

"How tiresome those people were! I thought we never should have got away from them," said Mrs. Beaumont. "What possessed them to come this morning, and to pay such a horrid long visit? Besides, those Duttons, at all times, are the most stupid creatures upon the face of the earth; I cannot endure them; so awkward and ill-bred too! and yet of a good family—who could think it? They are people one must see, but they are absolutely insufferable."

"Insufferable!" said Mr. Palmer; "why, my good madam, then you have the patience of a martyr; for you suffered them so patiently, that I never should have guessed you suffered at all. I protest I thought they were friends and favourites of yours, and that you were very glad to see them."

"Well, well, 'tis the way of the world," continued Mr. Palmer; "this sort of—what do you call it? double-dealing about visitors, goes on every where, Madam Beaumont. But how do I know, that when I go away, you may not be as glad to get rid of me as you were to get away from these Duttons?" added he, in a tone of forced jocularity. "How do I know, but that the minute my back is turned, you may not begin to take me to pieces in my turn, and say, 'That old Palmer! he was the most tiresome, humoursome, strange, old-fashioned fellow; I thought we should never have got rid of him?'"

"My dear, dear sir, how can you speak in such a manner?" cried Mrs. Beaumont, who had made several vain attempts to interrupt this speech. "You, who are our best friend! is it possible you could suspect? Is there no difference to be made between friends and common acquaintance?"

"I am sure I hope there is," said Mr. Palmer, smiling.

There was something so near the truth in Mr. Palmer's raillery, that Mrs. Beaumont could not take it with as much easy unconcern as the occasion required, especially in the presence of her son, who maintained a provoking silence. Unhappy indeed are those, who cannot, in such moments of distress, in their own families, and in their nearest connexions, find any relief from their embarrassments, and who look round in vain for one to be responsible for their sincerity. Mrs. Beaumont sat uneasy and almost disconcerted. Mr. Palmer felt for his snuff-box, his usual consolation; but it was not in his pocket: he had left it on his table. Now Mrs. Beaumont was relieved, for she had something to do, and something to say with her wonted politeness: in spite of all remonstrance from Mr. Palmer, her man Martin was sent back for the snuff-box; and conjectures about his finding it, and his being able to overtake them before they arrived at Walsingham house, supplied conversation for a mile or two.

"Here's Martin coming back full gallop, I vow," said Miss Hunter, who could also talk on this topic.

"Come, come, my good lady," said Mr. Palmer, (taking the moment when the young lady had turned her back as she stretched out of the carriage for the pleasure of seeing Martin gallop)—"Come, come, my good Mrs. Beaumont, shake hands and be friends, and hang the Duttons! I did not mean to vex you by what I said. I am not so polite as I should be, I know, and you perhaps are a little too polite. But that is no great harm, especially in a woman."

Martin and the snuff-box came up at this instant; and all was apparently as well as ever. Yet Mrs. Beaumont, who valued a reputation for sincerity as much as Chartres valued a reputation for honesty, and nearly upon the same principle, was seriously vexed that even this transient light had been let in upon her real character. To such accidents duplicity is continually subject.

CHAPTER IX

"Led by Simplicity divine,
She pleased, and never tried to shine;
She gave to chance each unschool'd feature,

And left her cause to sense and nature."
—MORE.

Arrived at Walsingham Park, they met Miss Walsingham walking at some distance from the house.

"Is Captain Walsingham come?" was the first question asked. "No, but expected every hour."

That he had not actually arrived was a comfortable reprieve to Mrs. Beaumont. Breathing more freely, and in refreshed spirits, she prepared to alight from her carriage, to walk to the house with Miss Walsingham, as Mr. Palmer proposed. Miss Hunter, who was dressed with uncommon elegance, remonstrated in favour of her delicate slippers: not that she named the real object of her solicitude—no; she had not spent so much time with Mrs. Beaumont, that great mistress of the art of apologizing, without learning at least the inferior practices of the trade. Of course she had all the little common arts of excuse ever ready: and instead of saying that she did not like to walk because she was afraid to spoil her shoes, she protested she was afraid of the heat, and could not walk so far. But Mr. Beaumont had jumped out of the carriage, and Mrs. Beaumont did not wish that he should walk home tête-à-tête with Miss Walsingham; therefore Miss Hunter's remonstrances were of no avail.

"My love, you, will not be heated, for our walk is through this charming shady grove; and if you are tired, here's my son will give you his arm."

Satisfied with this arrangement, the young lady, thus supported, found it possible to walk. Mr. Palmer walked his own pace, looking round at the beauties of the place, and desiring that nobody might mind him. This was his way, and Mrs. Beaumont never teased him with talking to him, when he did not seem to be in the humour for it. She, who made something of every thing, began to manage the conversation with her other companions during the walk, so as to favour her views upon the several parties. Pursuing her principle, that love is in men's minds generally independent of esteem, and believing that her son might be rendered afraid of the superiority of Miss Walsingham's understanding, Mrs. Beaumont took treacherous pains to draw her out. Starting from chance seemingly, as she well knew how, a subject of debate, she went from talking of the late marriage of some neighbouring couple, to discuss a question on which she believed that Miss Walsingham's opinion would differ from that of her son. The point was, whether a wife should or should not have pin-money. Miss Walsingham thought that a wife's accepting it would tend to establish a separate interest between married people. Mr. Beaumont, on the contrary, was of opinion, that a wife's having a separate allowance would prevent disputes. So Miss Hunter thought, of course, for she had been prepared to be precisely of Mr. Beaumont's opinion; but reasons she had none in its support. Indeed, she said with a pretty simper, she thought that women had nothing to do with reason or reasoning; that she thought a woman who really loved any body was always of that person's opinion; and especially in a wife she did not see of what use reasoning and all that could be, except to make a woman contradict, and be odd, and fond of ruling: that for her part she had no pretensions to any understanding, and if she had ever so much, she should be glad, she declared upon her honour, to get rid of it if she could; for what use could it possibly be of to her, when it must be the husband's understanding that must always judge and rule, and a wife ought only to obey, and be always of the opinion of the man of her choice?—Having thus made her profession of folly in broken sentences, with pretty confusion and all-becoming graces, she leaned upon Mr. Beaumont's arm with a bewitching air of languid delicacy, that solicited support. Mrs. Beaumont, suppressing a sigh, which, however, she took care that her son should hear, turned to Miss Walsingham, and, in a whisper, owned that she could not help loving abilities, and spirit too, even in her own sex. Then she observed aloud, that much might be urged on her side of the question with regard to pin-money; for not only, as Miss Walsingham justly said, it might tend to make a separate interest between husband and wife, but the wife would probably be kept in total ignorance of her husband's affairs; and that in some cases might be very disadvantageous, as some women are more capable, from their superior understanding, of managing every thing than most men, indeed, than any man she could name.

Even under favour of this pretty compliment, which was plainly directed by a glance of Mrs. Beaumont's eye, Miss Walsingham would not accept of this painful pre-eminence. She explained and made it clear, that she had not any ambition to rule or manage.

"That I can readily believe," said Mr. Beaumont; "for I have observed, that it is not always the women who are the most able to decide who are the most ambitious to govern."

This observation either was not heard or was not understood by Miss Hunter, whose whole soul was occupied in settling some fold of her drapery: but Mr. Beaumont's speech had its full effect on Mrs. Beaumont, who bit her lip, and looked reproachfully at her son, as if she thought this an infringement of his promised truce. A moment afterwards she felt the imprudence of her own reproachful look, and was sensible that she would have done better not to have fixed the opinion or feeling in her son's mind by noticing it thus with displeasure. Recovering, herself, for she never was disconcerted for more than half a minute, she passed on with easy grace to discuss the merits of the heroine of some new novel—an historic novel, which gave her opportunity of appealing to Miss Walsingham on some disputed points of history. She dexterously attempted to draw her well-informed young friend into a display of literature which might alarm Mr. Beaumont. His education had in some respects been shamefully neglected; for his mother had calculated that ignorance would ensure dependence. He had endeavoured to supply, at a late period of his education, the defects of its commencement; but he was sensible that he had not supplied all his deficiencies, and he was apt to feel, with painful impatient sensibility, his inferiority, whenever literary subjects were introduced. Miss Walsingham, however, was so perfectly free from all the affectation and vanity of a bel-esprit, that she did not alarm even those who were inferior to her in knowledge; their self-complacency, instead of being depressed by the comparison of their attainments with hers, was insensibly raised, by the perception that notwithstanding these, she could take pleasure in their conversation, could appreciate their good sense or originality of thought, without recurring to the authority of books, or of great names. In fact, her mind had never been overwhelmed by a wasteful torrent of learning. That the stream of literature had passed over, it was apparent only from its fertility. Mrs. Beaumont repented of having drawn her into conversation. Indeed, our heroine had trusted too much to some expressions, which had at times dropped from her son, about learned ladies, and certain conversaziones. She had concluded that he would never endure literature in a wife; but she now perceived her mistake. She discerned it too late; and at this moment she was doubly vexed, for she saw Miss Hunter produce herself in most disadvantageous contrast to her rival. In conformity to instructions, which Mrs. Beaumont had secretly given her, not to show too much sense or learning, because gentlemen in general, and in particular Mr. Beaumont, disliked it; this young lady now professed absolute ignorance and incapacity upon all subjects; and meaning to have an air of pretty childish innocence or timidity, really made herself appear quite like a simpleton. At the same time a tinge of ineffectual malice and envy appeared through her ill-feigned humility. She could give no opinion of any book—oh, she would not give any judgment for the whole world! She did not think herself qualified to speak, even if she had read the book, which indeed she had not, for, really, she never read—she was not a reading lady.

As Miss Hunter had no portion of Mrs. Beaumont's quick penetration, she did not see the unfavourable impression these words made: certain that she was following exactly her secret instructions, she was confident of being in the right line; so on she went, whilst Mrs. Beaumont sighed in vain; and Miss Walsingham, who now saw and understood her whole play, almost smiled at the comic of the scene.

"O dear, Mrs. Beaumont," continued Miss Hunter, "how can you ever appeal to me about books and those sorts of things, when you know I know nothing about the matter? For mercy's sake, never do so any more, for you know I've no taste for those sorts of things. And besides, I own, even if I could, I should so hate to be thought a blue-stocking—I would not have the least bit of blue in my stockings for the whole world—I'd rather have any other colour, black, white, red, green, yellow, any other colour. So I own I'm not sorry I'm not what they call a genius; for though genius to be sure's a very fascinating sort of thing in gentlemen, yet in women it is not so becoming, I think, especially in ladies: it does very well on the stage, and for artists, and so on; but really now, in company, I think it's an awkward thing, and would make one look so odd! Now, Mr. Beaumont, I must tell you an anecdote—"

"Stop, my dear Miss Hunter, your ear-ring is coming out. Stay! let me clasp it, love!" exclaimed Mrs. Beaumont, determined to stop her in the career of nonsense, by giving her sensations, since she could not give her ideas, a new turn.

"Oh, ma'am! ma'am! Oh! my ear! you are killing me, dearest Mrs. Beaumont! pinching me to death, ma'am!"

"Did I pinch, my dear? It was the hinge of the ear-ring, I suppose."

"I don't know what it was; but here's blood, I declare!"

"My love, I beg you a thousand pardons. How could I be so awkward! But why could not you for one moment hold your little head still?"

Miss Walsingham applied a patch to the wound.

"Such a pretty ear as it is," continued Mrs. Beaumont; "I am sure it was a pity to hurt it."

"You really did hurt it," said Mr. Beaumont, in a tone of compassion.

"Oh, horridly!" cried Miss Hunter—"and I, that always faint at the sight of blood!"

Afraid that the young lady would again spoil her part in the acting, and lose all the advantages which might result from the combined effect of the pretty ear and of compassion, Mrs. Beaumont endeavoured to take off her attention from the wound, by attacking her ear-rings.

"My love," said she, "don't wear these ear-rings any more, for I assure you there is no possibility of shutting or opening them, without hurting you."

This expedient, however, nearly proved fatal in its consequences. Miss Hunter entered most warmly into the defence of her ear-rings; and appealed to Mr. Beaumont to confirm her decision, that they were the prettiest and best ear-rings in the world. Unluckily, they did not particularly suit his fancy, and the young lady, who had, but half an hour before, professed that she could never be of a different opinion in any thing from that of the man she loved, now pettishly declared that she could not and would not give up her taste. Incensed still more by a bow of submission, but not of conviction, from Mr. Beaumont, she went on regardless of her dearest Mrs. Beaumont's frowns, and vehemently maintained her judgment, quoting, with triumphant volubility, innumerable precedents of ladies, "who had just bought the very same ear-rings, and whose taste she believed nobody would dispute."

Mr. Beaumont had seen enough, now and upon many other occasions, to be convinced that it is not on matters of consequence that ladies are apt to grow most angry; and he stood confirmed in his belief that those who in theory professed to have such a humble opinion of their own abilities that they cannot do or understand any thing useful, are often, in practice, the most prone to insist upon the infallibility of their taste and judgment. Mrs. Beaumont, who saw with one glance of her quick eye what passed at this moment in her son's mind, sighed, and said to herself—"How impossible to manage a fool, who ravels, as fast as one weaves, the web of her fortune!"

Yet though Mrs. Beaumont perceived and acknowledged the impracticability of managing a fool for a single hour, it was one of the favourite objects of her manoeuvres to obtain this very fool for a daughter-in-law, with the hope of governing her for life. So inconsistent are cunning people, even of the best abilities; so ill do they calculate the value of their ultimate objects, however ingeniously they devise their means, or adapt them to their ends.

During this walk Mr. Palmer had taken no part in the conversation; he had seemed engrossed with his own thoughts, or occupied with observing the beauties of the place. Tired with her walk—for Mrs. Beaumont always complained of being fatigued when she was vexed, thus at once concealing her vexation, and throwing the faults of her mind upon her body—she stretched herself upon a sofa as soon as she reached the house, nor did she recover from her exhausted state till she cast her eyes upon a tamborine, which she knew would afford means of showing Miss Hunter's figure and graces to advantage. Slight as this resource may seem, Mrs. Beaumont well knew that slighter still have often produced great effects. Soon afterward she observed her son smile repeatedly as he read a passage in some book that lay upon the table, and she had the curiosity to take up the book when he turned away. She found that it was Cumberland's Memoirs, and saw the following little poem marked with reiterated lines of approbation:

"Why, Affectation, why this mock grimace? Go, silly thing, and hide that simp'ring face. Thy lisping prattle, and thy mincing gait, All thy false mimic fooleries I hate; For thou art Folly's counterfeit, and she Who is right foolish hath the better plea; Nature's true idiot I prefer to thee.   Why that soft languish? Why that drawling tone? Art sick, art sleepy? Get thee hence: begone. I laugh at all thy pretty baby tears, Those flutt'rings, faintings, and unreal fears.   Can they deceive us? Can such mumm'ries move, Touch us with pity, or inspire with love? No, Affectation, vain is all thy art! Those eyes may wander over ev'ry part; They'll never find their passage to the heart." Mrs. Beaumont, the moment she had read these lines, perceived why her son had smiled. The portrait seemed really to have been drawn from Miss Hunter, and the lines were so à propos to the scene which had just passed during the walk, that it was impossible to avoid the application. Mrs. Beaumont shut the book hastily as her dear Albina approached, for she was afraid that the young lady would have known her own picture. So few people, however, even of those much wiser than Miss Hunter, know themselves, that she need not have been alarmed. But she had no longer leisure to devote her thoughts to this subject, for Mr. Walsingham, who had been out riding, had by this time returned; and the moment he entered the room, Mrs. Beaumont's attention was directed to him and to Mr. Palmer. She introduced them to each other, with many expressions of regret that they should not sooner have met.

Characters that are free from artifice immediately coalesce, as metals that are perfectly pure can be readily cemented together. Mr. Palmer and Mr. Walsingham were intimate in half an hour. There was an air of openness and sincerity about Mr. Walsingham; a freedom and directness in his conversation, which delighted Mr. Palmer.

"I am heartily glad we have met at last, my good cousin Walsingham," said he: "very sorry should I have been to have left the country without becoming acquainted with you: and now I wish your gallant captain was arrived. I am to set off the day after to-morrow, and I am sadly afraid I shall miss seeing him."

Mr. Walsingham said, that as they expected him every hour, he hoped Mr. Palmer would persuade Mrs. Beaumont to spend the day at Walsingham House.

Mrs. Beaumont dared not object. On the contrary, it was now her policy to pretend the fondest friendship for all the Walsingham family: yet, all the time, pursuing her plan of preventing Mr. Palmer from discerning their real characters and superior merit, she managed with great dexterity to keep the conversation as much as possible upon general topics, and tried to prevent Mr. Palmer from being much alone with Mr. Walsingham, for she dreaded their growing intimacy. After dinner, however, when the ladies retired, the gentlemen drew their chairs close together, and had a great deal of conversation on interesting subjects. The most interesting was Captain Walsingham: Mr. Palmer earnestly desired to hear the particulars of his history.

"And from whom," said young Beaumont, turning to Mr. Walsingham, "can he hear them better than from Captain Walsingham's guardian and friend?"

CHAPTER X

"Yet never seaman more serenely brave
Led Britain's conquering squadrons o'er the wave."

"Friends are not always the best biographers," said Mr. Walsingham; "but I will try to be impartial. My ward's first desire to be a sailor was excited, as he has often since told me, by reading Robinson Crusoe. When he was scarcely thirteen he went out in the Resolute, a frigate, under the command of Captain Campbell. Campbell was an excellent officer, and very strict in all that related to order and discipline. It was his principle and his practice never to forgive a first offence; by which the number of second faults was considerably diminished. My ward was not much pleased at first with his captain; but he was afterwards convinced that this strictness was what made a man of him. He was buffeted about, and shown the rough of life; made to work hard, and submit to authority. To reason he was always ready to yield; and by degrees he learned that his first duty as a sailor was implicit obedience. In due time he was made lieutenant: in this situation, his mixed duties of command and obedience were difficult, because his first-lieutenant, the captain's son, was jealous of him.

"Walsingham found it a more difficult task to win the confidence of the son than it had been to earn the friendship of the father. His punctuality in obeying orders, and his respectful manner to the lieutenant, availed but little; for young Campbell still viewed him with scornful yet with jealous eyes, imagining that he only wanted to show himself the better officer.

"Of the falsehood of these suspicions Walsingham had at last an opportunity of giving unquestionable proof. It happened one day that Lieutenant Campbell, impatient at seeing a sailor doing some work awkwardly on the outside of the vessel, snatched the rope from his hand, and swore he would do it himself. In his hurry, Campbell missed his footing, and fell overboard:—he could not swim. Walsingham had the presence of mind to order the ship to be put about, and plunged instantly into the water to save his rival. With much exertion he reached Campbell, supported him till the boat was lowered down, and got him safe aboard again."

"Just like himself!" cried young Beaumont; "all he ever wanted was opportunity to show his soul."

"The first-lieutenant's jealousy was now changed into gratitude," continued Mr. Walsingham; "and from this time forward, instead of suffering from that petty rivalship by which he used to be obstructed, Walsingham enjoyed the entire confidence of young Campbell. This good understanding between him and his brother officer not only made their every day lives pleasant, but in times of difficulty secured success. For three years that they lived together after this period, and during which time they were ordered to every quarter of the globe, they never had the slightest dispute, either in the busiest or the idlest times. At length, in some engagement with a Dutch ship, the particulars of which I forget, Lieutenant Campbell was mortally wounded: his last words were—'Walsingham, comfort my father.' That was no easy task. Stern as Captain Campbell seemed, the loss of his son was irreparable. He never shed a tear when he was told it was all over, but said, 'God's will be done;' and turning into his cabin, desired to be left alone. Half an hour afterwards he sent for Walsingham, who found him quite calm. 'We must see and do our duty together to the last,' said he.

"He exerted himself strenuously, and to all outward appearance was, as the sailors said, the same man as ever; but Walsingham, who knew him better, saw that his heart was broken, and that he wished for nothing but an honourable death. One morning as he was on deck looking through his glass, he called to Walsingham; 'Your eyes are better than mine,' said he; 'look here, and tell me, do you see yonder sail—she's French? Le Magnanime frigate, if I'm not mistaken. 'Yes,' said Walsingham, 'I know her by the patch in her main sail.'—'We'll give her something to do,' said Campbell, 'though she's so much our superior. Please God, before the sun's over our heads, you shall have her in tow, Walsingham.' 'We shall, I trust,' said Walsingham.—'Perhaps not we; for I own I wish to fall,' said Campbell. 'You are first-lieutenant now; I can't leave my men under better command, and I hope the Admiralty will give you the ship, if you give it to his Majesty.'—Then turning to the sailors, Captain Campbell addressed them with a countenance unusually cheerful; and, after a few words of encouragement, gave orders to clear decks for action. 'Walsingham, you'll see to every thing whilst I step down to write.' He wrote, as it was afterwards found, two letters, both concerning Walsingham's interests. The frigate with which they had to engage was indeed far superior to them in force; but Campbell trusted to the good order and steadiness as well as to the courage of his men. The action was long and obstinate. Twice the English attempted to board the enemy, and twice were repulsed. The third time, just as Captain Campbell had seized hold of the French colours, which hung in rags over the side of the enemy's ship, he received a wound in his breast, fell back into Walsingham's arms, and almost instantly expired. The event of this day was different from what Campbell had expected, for Le Succès of fifty guns appeared in sight; and, after a desperate engagement with her, in which Walsingham was severely wounded, and every other officer on board killed or wounded, Walsingham saw that nothing was left but to make a wanton sacrifice of the remainder of his crew, or to strike.

"After a contest of six hours, he struck to Le Succès. Perfect silence on his deck; a loud and insulting shout from the enemy!

"No sooner had Walsingham struck, than La Force, the captain of Le Succès hailed him, and ordered him to come in his own boat, and to deliver his sword. Walsingham replied, that 'his sword, so demanded, should never be delivered but with his life.'2 The Frenchman did not think proper to persist; but soon after sent his lieutenant on board the Resolute, where the men were found at their quarters with lighted matches in their hands, ready to be as good as their word. La Force, the captain of Le Succès, was a sailor of fortune, who had risen by chance, not merit."

"Ay, ay," interrupted Mr. Palmer, "so I thought; and there was no great merit, or glory either, in a French fifty gun taking an English frigate, after standing a six hours' contest with another ship. Well, my dear sir, what became of poor Walsingham? How did this rascally Frenchman treat his prisoners?"

"Scandalously!" cried Beaumont; "and yet Walsingham is so generous that he will never let me damn the nation, for what he says was only the fault of an individual, who disgraced it."

"Well, let me hear and judge for myself," said Mr. Palmer.

"La Force carried the Resolute in triumph into a French port," continued Mr. Walsingham. "Vain of displaying his prisoners, he marched them up the country, under pretence that they would not be safe in a sea-port. Cambray was the town in which they were confined. Walsingham found the officers of the garrison very civil to him at first; but when they saw that he was not fond of high play, and that he declined being of their parties at billiards and vingt-un, they grew tired of him; for without these resources they declared they should perish with ennui in a country town. Even under the penalty of losing all society, Walsingham resisted every temptation to game, and submitted to live with the strictest economy rather than to run in debt."

"But did you never send him any money? Or did not he get your remittances?" said Mr. Palmer.

"My dear sir, by some delays of letters, we did not hear for two months where he was imprisoned."

"And he was reduced to the greatest distress," pursued Beaumont; "for he had shared all he had, to the utmost farthing, with his poor fellow-prisoners."

"Like a true British sailor!" said Mr. Palmer. "Well, sir, I hope he contrived to make his escape?"

"No, for he would not break his parole," said Beaumont,

"His parole! I did not know he was on his parole," said Mr. Palmer. "Then certainly he could not break it."

"He had two tempting opportunities, I can assure you," said Beaumont; "one offered by the commandant's lady, who was not insensible to his merit; the other, by the gratitude of some poor servant, whom he had obliged—Mr. Walsingham can tell you all the particulars."

"No, I need not detail the circumstances; it is enough to tell you, sir, that he withstood the temptations, would not break his parole, and remained four months a prisoner in Cambray. Like the officers of the garrison, he should have drunk or gamed, or else he must have died of vexation, he says, if he had not fortunately had a taste for reading, and luckily procured books from a good old priest's library. At the end of four months the garrison of Cambray was changed; and instead of a set of dissipated officers, there came a well-conducted regiment, under the command of M. de Villars, an elderly officer of sense and discretion."

"An excellent man!" cried Beaumont: "I love him with all my soul, though I never saw him. But I beg your pardon for interrupting you, Mr. Walsingham."

"A prattling hairdresser at Cambray first prepossessed M. de Villars in Walsingham's favour, by relating a number of anecdotes intended to throw abuse and ridicule upon the English captain, to convict him of misanthropy and economy; of having had his hair dressed but twice since he came to Cambray; of never having frequented the society of Madame la Marquise de Marsillac, the late commandant's lady, for more than a fortnight after his arrival, and of having actually been detected in working with his own hand with smiths' and carpenters' tools. Upon the strength of the hairdresser's information, M. de Villars paid the English captain a visit; was pleased by his conversation, and by all that he observed of his conduct and character.

"As M. de Villars was going down stairs, after having spent an evening with Walsingham, a boy of twelve years old, the son of the master of the lodging-house, equipped in a military uniform, stood across the landing-place, as if determined to, stop him. 'Mon petit militaire,' said the commandant, 'do you mean to dispute my passage?' 'Non, mon général,' said the boy; 'I know my duty too well. But I post myself here to demand an audience, for I have a secret of importance to communicate.' M. de Villars, smiling at the boy's air of consequence, yet pleased with the steady earnestness of his manner, took him by the hand into an antechamber, and said that he was ready to listen to whatever he had to impart. The boy then told him that he had accidentally overheard a proposal which had been made to facilitate the English captain's escape, and that the captain refused to comply with it, because it was not honourable to break his parole. The boy, who had been struck by the circumstance, and who, besides, was grateful to Walsingham for some little instances of kindness, spoke with much enthusiasm in his favour; and, as M. de Villars afterwards repeated, finished his speech by exclaiming, 'I would give every thing I have in the world, except my sword and my honour, to procure this English captain his liberty.'

"M. de Villars was pleased with the boy's manner, and with the fact which he related; so much so, that he promised, that if Walsingham's liberty could be obtained he would procure it. 'And you, my good little friend, shall, if I succeed,' added he, 'have the pleasure of being the first to tell him the good news.'

"Some days afterwards, the boy burst into Walsingham's room, exclaiming, 'Liberty! liberty! you are at liberty!'—He danced and capered with such wild joy, that it was some time before Walsingham could obtain any explanation, or could prevail on him to let him look at a letter which he held in his hand, flourishing it about in triumph. At last he showed that it was an order from M. de Villars, for the release of Captain Walsingham, and of all the English prisoners, belonging to the Resolute, for whom exchanges had been effected. No favour could be granted in a manner more honourable to all the parties concerned. Walsingham arrived in England without any farther difficulties."

"Thank God!" said Mr. Palmer. "Well, now he has touched English ground again, I have some hopes for him. What next?"

"The first thing he did, of course, was to announce his return to the Admiralty. A court-martial was held at Portsmouth; and, fortunately for him, was composed of officers of the highest distinction, so that the first men in his profession became thoroughly acquainted with the circumstances of his conduct. The enthusiasm with which his men bore testimony in his favour was gratifying to his feelings, and the minutes of the evidence were most honourable to him. The court pronounced, that Lieutenant Walsingham had done all that could be effected by the most gallant and judicious officer in the defence of His Majesty's ship Resolute. The ministry who had employed Captain Campbell were no longer in place, and one of the Lords of the Admiralty at this time happened to have had some personal quarrel with him. A few days after the trial, Walsingham was at a public dinner, at which Campbell's character became the subject of conversation. Walsingham was warned, in a whisper, that the first Lord of the Admiralty's private secretary was present, and was advised to be prudent; but Walsingham's prudence was not of that sort which can coolly hear a worthy man's memory damned with faint praise; his prudence was not of that sort which can tamely sit by and see a friend's reputation in danger. With all the warmth and eloquence of friendship, he spoke in Captain Campbell's defence, and paid a just and energetic tribute of praise to his memory. He spoke, and not a word more was said against Campbell. The politicians looked down upon their plates; and there was a pause of that sort, which sometimes in a company of interested men of the world results from surprise at the imprudent honesty of a good-natured novice. Walsingham, as the company soon afterwards broke up, heard one gentleman say of him to another, as they went away, 'There's a fellow now, who has ruined himself without knowing it, and all for a dead man.' It was not without knowing it: Walsingham was well aware what he hazarded, but he was then, and ever, ready to sacrifice his own interests in the defence of truth and of a friend. For two long years afterwards, Walsingham was, in the technical and elegant phrase, left on the shelf, and the door of promotion was shut against him."

"Yes, and there he might have remained till now," said Beaumont, "if it had not been for that good Mr. Gaspar, a clerk in one of their offices; a man who, though used to live among courtiers and people hackneyed in the political ways of the world, was a plain, warm-hearted friend, a man of an upright character, who prized integrity and generosity the more because he met with them so seldom. But I beg your pardon, Mr. Walsingham; will you go on and tell Mr. Palmer how and why Gaspar served our friend?"

"One day Walsingham had occasion to go to Mr. Gaspar's office to search for some papers relative to certain charts which he had drawn, and intended to present to the Admiralty. In talking of the soundings of some bay he had taken whilst out with Captain Campbell, he mentioned him, as he always did, with terms of affection and respect. Mr. Gaspar immediately asked, 'Are you, sir, that Lieutenant Walsingham, of the Resolute, who at a public dinner about two years ago made such a disinterested defence of your captain? If it is in my power to serve you, depend upon it I will. Leave your charts with me; I think I may have an opportunity of turning them to your advantage, and that of the service.' Gaspar, who was thoroughly in earnest, took a happy moment to present Walsingham's charts before the Admiralty, just at a time when they were wanted. The Admiralty were glad to employ an officer who had some local information, and they sent him out in the Dreadnought, a thirty-six gun frigate, with Captain Jemmison, to the West Indies."

"And what sort of a man was his new captain?" said Mr. Palmer.

"As unlike his old one as possible," said Beaumont.

"Yes," continued Mr. Walsingham; "in every point, except courage, Captain Jemmison was as complete a contrast as could be imagined to Captain Campbell. Whatever else he might be, Jemmison was certainly a man of undaunted courage."

"That's of course, if he was a captain in the British navy," said Mr. Palmer.

"From his appearance, however, you would never have taken him for a gallant sailor," said Mr. Walsingham: "abhorring the rough, brutal, swearing, grog-drinking, tobacco-chewing, race of sea-officers, the Bens and the Mirvans of former times, Captain Jemmison, resolving, I suppose, to avoid their faults, went into the contrary extreme of refinement and effeminacy. A superlative coxcomb, and an epicure more from fashion than taste, he gloried in descanting, with technical precision, on the merits of dishes and of cooks. His table, even on shipboard, was to be equalled in elegance only by his toilet."

"The puppy!" exclaimed Mr. Palmer. "And how could Captain Walsingham go on with such a coxcomb?"

"Very ill, you may be sure," said Beaumont; "for Walsingham, I'll answer for it, never could conceal or control his feelings of contempt or indignation."

"Yet, as Captain Jemmison's lieutenant, he always behaved with perfect propriety," said Mr. Walsingham, "and bore with his foppery and impertinence with the patience becoming a subordinate officer to his superior. Jemmison could not endure a lieutenant whose character and manners were a continual contrast and reproach to his own, and he disliked him the more because he could never provoke him to any disrespect. Jemmison often replied even to Walsingham's silent contempt; as a French pamphleteer once published a book entitled, Réponse au Silence de M. de la Motte. On some points, where duty and principle were concerned, Walsingham, however, could not be silent. There was a lad of the name of Birch on board the Dreadnought, whom Walsingham had taken under his immediate care, and whom he was endeavouring to train up in every good habit. Jemmison, to torment Walsingham, made it his pleasure to counteract him in these endeavours, and continually did all he could to spoil Birch by foolish indulgence. Walsingham's indignation was upon these occasions vehement, and his captain and he came to frequent quarrels. Young Birch, who had sense enough to know which was his true friend, one day threw himself on his knees to beseech his lieutenant not to hazard so much on his account, and solemnly swore that he would never be guilty of the slightest excess or negligence during the remainder of the voyage. The young man was steady to his promise, and by his resolution and temper prevented Walsingham and his captain from coming to a serious rupture. When they arrived at their place of destination, Jamaica, Captain Jemmison went on shore to divert himself, and spent his time in great dissipation at Spanish Town, eating, dressing, dancing, gallanting, and glorying in its being observed by all the ladies that he had nothing of a sea-captain about him. The other officers, encouraged by his precept and example, left the ship; but Walsingham stayed on board, and had severe duty to perform, for he could not allow the crew to go on shore, because they got into riots with the townspeople. Soon after their arrival, and even during the course of their voyage, he had observed among the sailors something like a disposition to mutiny, encouraged probably by the negligence and apparent effeminacy of their captain. Though they knew him to be a man of intrepidity, yet they ridiculed and despised his coxcombry, and his relaxation of discipline gave them hopes of succeeding in their mutinous schemes. Walsingham strongly and repeatedly represented to Captain Jemmison the danger, and remonstrated with him and the other officers upon the imprudence of leaving the ship at this juncture; but Jemmison, in a prettily rounded period, protested he saw no penumbra of danger, and that till he was called upon by Mars, he owned he preferred the charms of Venus.

"This was vastly elegant; but, nevertheless, it happened one night, when the captain, after having eaten an admirable supper, was paying his court to a Creole lady of Spanish Town, news was brought him, that the crew of the Dreadnought had mutinied, and that Lieutenant Walsingham was killed. One half of the report was true, and the other nearly so. At midnight, after having been exhausted during the preceding week by his vigilance, Walsingham had just thrown himself into his cot, when he was roused by Birch at his cabin-door, crying, 'A mutiny! a mutiny on deck!'—Walsingham seized his drawn cutlass, and ran up the ladder, determined to cut down the ringleader; but just as he reached the top, the sailors shut down the hatchway, which struck his head with such violence, that he fell, stunned, and, to all appearance, dead. Birch contrived, in the midst of the bustle, before he was himself seized by the mutineers, to convey, by signals to shore, news of what had happened. But Captain Jemmison could now be of no use. Before he could take any measures to prevent them, the mutineers weighed anchor, and the Dreadnought, under a brisk breeze, was out of the bay; all the other vessels in the harbour taking it for granted that her captain was on board, and that she was sailing under orders. In the mean time, whilst Walsingham was senseless, the sailors stowed him into his cabin, and set a guard over him. The ringleader, Jefferies, a revengeful villain, who bore malice against him for some just punishment, wanted to murder him, but the rest would not consent. Some would not dip their hands in blood; others pleaded for him, and said that he was never cruel. One man urged, that the lieutenant had been kind to him when he was sick. Another suggested, that it would be well to keep him alive to manage the ship for them, in case of difficulties. Conscious of their ignorance, they acceded to this advice; Jefferies' proposal to murder him was overruled: and it was agreed to keep Walsingham close prisoner till they should need his assistance. He had his timekeeper and log-book locked up with him, which were totally forgotten by these miscreants. Never seaman prayed more fervently for fair weather than Walsingham now did for a storm. At last, one night he heard (and he says it was one of the pleasantest sounds he ever heard in his life) the wind rising. Soon it blew a storm. He heard one of the sailors say—'A stiff gale, Jack!' and another—'An ugly night!' Presently, great noise on deck, and the pumps at work. Every moment he now expected a deputation from the mutineers. The first person he saw was the carpenter, who came in to knock in the dead lights in the cabin windows. The man was surly, and would give no answer to any questions; but Walsingham knew, by the hurry of his work, that the fellow thought there was no time to be lost. Twice, before he could finish what he was about, messages came from Captain Jefferies, to order him to something else. Then a violent crash above from the fall of a mast; and then he heard one cry—'I'll be cursed if I should care, if we did but know where-abouts we are.' Then all was in such uproar, that no voices could be distinguished. At last his cabin-door unlocked, and many voices called upon him at once to come upon deck that instant and save the ship. Walsingham absolutely refused to do any thing for them till they returned to their duty, delivered up to him their arms, and their ringleader, Jefferies. At this answer they stood aghast. Some tried entreaties, some threats: all in vain. Walsingham coolly said, he would go to the bottom along with the ship rather than say a word to save them, till they submitted. The storm blew stronger—the danger every moment increasing. One of the mutineers came with a drawn cutlass, another levelled a blunderbuss at Walsingham, swearing to despatch him that instant, if he would not tell them where they were. 'Murder me, and you will be hanged; persist in your mutiny, you'll be drowned,' said Walsingham. 'You'll never make me swerve from my duty—and you know it—you have my answer.' The enraged sailors seized him in their arms, and carried him by force upon deck, where the sight of the danger, and the cries of 'Throw him overboard!—over with him!' only seemed to fortify his resolution. Not a word, not a sign could they get from him. The rudder was now unshipped! At this the sailors' fury turned suddenly upon Jefferies, who between terror and ignorance was utterly incapacitated. They seized, bound, gave him up to

Walsingham, returned to their duty; and then, and not till then, Walsingham resumed his command. Walsingham's voice, once more heard, inspired confidence, and with the hopes revived the exertions of the sailors. I am not seaman enough to tell you how the ship was saved; but that it was saved, and saved by Walsingham, is certain. I remember only, that he made the ship manageable by some contrivance, which he substituted in the place of the rudder that had been unshipped. The storm abating, he made for the first port, to repair the ship's damages, intending to return to Jamaica, to deliver her up to her captain; but, from a vessel they spoke at sea, he learned that Jemmison was gone to England in a merchantman. To England then Walsingham prepared to follow."

"And with this rebel crew!" cried Beaumont; "think, Mr. Palmer, what a situation he was in, knowing, as he did, that every rascal of them would sooner go to the devil than go home, where they knew they must be tried for their mutiny."

"Well, sir, well!" said Mr. Palmer. "Did they run away with the ship a second time? or how did he manage?"

He called them all one morning together on deck; and pointing to the place where the gunpowder was kept, he said—'I have means of blowing up the ship. If ever you attempt to mutiny again, the first finger you lay upon me, I blow her up instantly.' They had found him to be a man of resolution. They kept to their duty. Not a symptom of disobedience during the rest of the voyage. In their passage they fell in with an enemy's ship, far superior to them in force. 'There, my lads!' said Walsingham, 'if you have a mind to earn your pardons, there's your best chance. Take her home with you to your captain and your king.' A loud cheer was their answer. They fought like devils to redeem themselves. Walsingham—but without stopping to make his panegyric, I need only tell you, that Walsingham's conduct and intrepidity were this time crowned with success. He took the enemy's ship, and carried it in triumph into Portsmouth. Jemmison was on the platform when they came in; and what a mortifying sight it was to him, and what a proud hour to Walsingham, you may imagine! Having delivered the Dreadnought and her prize over to his captain, the next thing to be thought of was the trial of the mutineers. All except Jefferies obtained a pardon, in consideration of their return to duty, and their subsequent services. Jefferies was hanged at the yard-arm. The trial of the mutineers brought on, as Jemmison foresaw it must, many animadversions on his own conduct. Powerful connexions, and his friends in place, silenced, as much as possible, the public voice. Jemmison gave excellent dinners, and endeavoured to drown the whole affair in his choice Champagne and London particular Madeira; so his health, and success to the British navy, was drunk in bumper toasts.

"Ay, ay, they think to do every thing now in England by dinners, and bumper toasts, and three times three," said Mr. Palmer.

"But it did not do in this instance," said Beaumont, in a tone of exultation: "it did not do."

"No," continued Mr. Walsingham; "though Jemmison's dinners went down vastly well with a party, they did not satisfy the public. The opposition papers grew clamorous, and the business was taken up so strongly, and it raised such a cry against the ministry, that they were obliged to bring Jemmison to a court-martial."

"The puppy! I'm glad of it, with all my soul. And how did he look then?" said Mr. Palmer.

"Vastly like a gentleman; that was all that even his friends could say for him. The person he was most afraid of on the trial was Walsingham. In this apprehension he was confirmed by certain of his friends, who had attempted to sound Walsingham as to the nature of the evidence he intended to give. They all reported, that they could draw nothing out of him, and that he was an impracticable fellow; for his constant answer was, that his evidence should be given in court, and nowhere else."

"Even to his most intimate friends," interrupted Mr. Beaumont, "even to me, who was in the house with him all the time the trial was going on, he did not tell what his evidence would be."

"When the day of trial came," pursued Mr. Walsingham—

"Don't forget Admiral Dashleigh," said Mr. Beaumont.

"No; who can forget him that knows him?" said Walsingham: "a warm, generous friend, open-hearted as he is brave—he came to Captain Walsingham the day before the court-martial was to sit. 'I know, Walsingham, you don't like my cousin Jemmison (said he), nor do I much, for he is a puppy, and I never could like a puppy, related to me or not; be that as it may, you'll do him justice, I'm sure; for though he is a puppy he is a brave fellow—and here, for party purposes, they have raised a cry of his being a coward, and want to shoot him pour encourager les autres. What you say will damn or save him; and I have too good an opinion of you to think that any old grudge, though you might have cause for it, would stand in his way.' Walsingham answered as usual, that his opinion and his evidence would be known on the day of trial. Dashleigh went away very ill-satisfied, and persuaded that Walsingham harboured revenge against his relation. At last, when he was called upon in court, Walsingham's conduct was both just and generous; for though his answers spoke the exact truth, yet he brought forward nothing to the disadvantage of Jemmison, but what truth compelled him to state, and in his captain's favour; on the contrary, he spoke so strongly of his intrepidity, and of the gallant actions which in former instances he had performed in the service, as quite to efface the recollection of his foppery and epicurism, and, as much as possible, to excuse his negligence. Walsingham's evidence absolutely confuted the unjust charge or suspicion of cowardice that had been raised against Jemmison; and made such an impression in his favour, that, instead of being dismissed the service, or even having his ship taken from him, as was expected, Jemmison got off with a reprimand."

"Which I am sure he well deserved," said Mr. Palmer.

"But certainly Walsingham was right not to let him be run down by a popular cry, especially as he had used him ill," said Mr. Beaumont.

"Well, well!—I don't care about the puppy," cried Mr. Palmer; "only go on."

"No sooner was the trial over, and the sentence of the court made known, than Admiral Dashleigh, full of joy, admiration, and gratitude, pushed his way towards Walsingham, and stretching out his hand, exclaimed—'Shake hands, Walsingham, and forgive me, or I can't forgive myself. I suspected you yesterday morning of bearing malice against that coxcomb, who deserved to be laughed at, but not to be shot. By Jove, Walsingham, you're an honest fellow, I find.' 'And have you but just found that out, admiral?' said Walsingham, with a proud smile. 'Harkee, my lad,' said Dashleigh, calling after him, 'remember, I'm your friend, at all events.—Take it as you will, I'll make you mine yet, before I've done with you.' Walsingham knew that at this time Admiral Dashleigh's friends were in power, and that Dashleigh himself had great influence with the Admiralty; and he probably treated the admiral thus haughtily, to show that he had no interested views or hopes. Dashleigh understood this, for he now comprehended Walsingham's character perfectly. Immediately after the trial, Walsingham was made commander, in consequence of his having saved the Dreadnought, and his having taken l'Ambuscade. With this appointment Dashleigh had nothing to do. But he never ceased exerting himself, employing all the interest of his high connexions, and all the personal influence of his great abilities, to have Walsingham made post, and to get him a ship. He succeeded at last; but he never gave the least hint that it was done by his interest; for, he said, he knew that Walsingham had such nice notions, and was such a proud principled fellow, that he would not enjoy his promotion, if he thought he owed it to any thing upon earth but his own merit. So a handsome letter was written by the secretary of the Admiralty to Captain Walsingham, by their lordships' desire, informing him, 'that in consideration of his services and merit, his majesty had been pleased to make him post-captain, and to appoint him to the command of l'Ambuscade (the prize he took), which would be sent out on the first occasion.' The secretary 'begged leave to add expressions of his private satisfaction on an appointment so likely to be advantageous to the public,' &c. In short, it was all done so properly and so plausibly, that even Walsingham never suspected any secret influence, nor did he find out the part Dashleigh had taken in the business till several months afterwards, when a discreet friend mentioned it by accident."

"I was that discreet friend," said Mr. Beaumont.

"Well, all this is very good, but there's no love in this Story," said Mr. Palmer. "I hope your hero is not too proud to fall in love?"

"Too proud!—We are told, you know, that the greatest hero, in the intervals of war, resigned

'To tender passions all his mighty mind.'"

"Tender passions!—Captain Walsingham is in love, then, hey?" said Mr. Palmer. "And may I ask—Bless me! I shall be very sorry if it is with any body but—may I ask to whom he is attached?"

"That is a question that I am not quite at liberty perhaps to answer," said Mr. Walsingham. "During the interval between his return in the Dreadnought and his being appointed to l'Ambuscade, an interval of about eighteen months, which he spent in the country here with me, he had time to become thoroughly acquainted with a very amiable young lady—"

"A very amiable young lady! and in this neighbourhood?" interrupted Mr. Palmer; "it must be the very person I mean, the very person I wish."

"Do not ask me any more," said Mr. Walsingham; "for my friend never declared his attachment, and I have no right to declare it for him. He was not, at the time I speak of, in circumstances to marry; therefore he honourably concealed, or rather suppressed, his passion, resolving not to attempt to engage the young lady's affections till he should have made a fortune sufficient to support her in her own rank in life."

"Well, now, that's all done, thank Heaven!" cried Palmer: "he has fortune enough now, or we can help him out, you know. This is excellent, excellent!—Come, is it not time for us to go to the ladies? I'm impatient to tell this to Mrs. Beaumont."

"Stay, my good Mr. Palmer," said Mr. Walsingham. "What are you going to do?"

"Let me alone, let me alone—I'll only tell what I guess—depend upon it, I guess right—and it may do a great deal of good to tell it to Mrs. Beaumont, and it will give her a great deal of pleasure—trust me—trust me."

"I do trust you—but perhaps you may be mistaken."

"Not at all, not at all, depend upon it; so let me go to her this minute."

"But stop, my dear sir," cried Mr. Beaumont, "stop for another reason; let me beg you to sit down again—I am not clear that Captain Walsingham is not at this instant in love with—perhaps, as it is reported, married to a Spanish lady, whom he has carried off out of a convent at —, and whom I understand he is bringing home with him."

"Heyday! a Spanish lady!" said Mr. Palmer, returning slowly to his seat with a fallen countenance. "How's this?—By St. George, this is unlucky! But how's this, I say?"

"You did not let us finish our story," said Mr. Beaumont, "or we should have told you."

"Let me hear the end of it now," said Mr. Palmer, sitting down again, and preparing himself with several pinches of snuff. But just at this instant a servant came to say that coffee was ready.

"I will never stir from this spot for coffee or any thing else," said Mr. Palmer, "till I know the history of the Spanish lady."

"Then the shortest and best way I have of telling it to you is, to beg you to read this letter, which contains all I know of the matter," said Mr. Beaumont. "This letter is from young Birch to his parents; we have never heard a syllable directly from Walsingham himself on this subject. Since he reached Lisbon, we have had no letters from him, except that short epistle which brought us an account of his taking the treasure-ship. But we shall see him soon, and know the truth of this story; and hear whether he prefers his Spanish or his English mistress."

"'Fore George! I wish this Spanish woman had stayed in her convent," said Mr. Palmer; "I don't like runaway ladies. But let us see what this letter says for her."

The letter is the same that Mr. Beaumont read some time ago, therefore it need not here be inserted. Before Mr. Palmer had finished perusing it, a second message came to say that the ladies waited tea, and that Mrs. Beaumont wished not to be late going home, as there was no moon. Mr. Palmer, nevertheless, finished the letter before he stirred: and then, with a heavy sigh, he rose and said, "I now wish, more than ever, that our captain would come home this night, before I go, and clear up this business. I don't like this Spanish plot, this double intrigue. Ah, dear me!—I shall be obliged to sail—I shall be in Jamaica before the fifth act."

"How expectation loads the wings of time!" exclaimed Mrs. Beaumont, as the gentlemen entered the drawing-room. "Here we have been all day expecting our dear Captain Walsingham, and the time has seemed so long!—The only time I ever found long in this house."

"I should like to know," said Mr. Walsingham, after a bow of due acknowledgment to Mrs. Beaumont for her compliment, "I should like to know whether time appears to pass more slowly to those that hope, or those that fear?"

Mrs. Beaumont handed coffee to Mr. Palmer, without attempting to answer this question.

"To those that hope, I should think," said Mr. Palmer; "for hope long deferred maketh the heart sick; and time can answer for it, passes most slowly to those who are sick."

"'Slow as the year's dull circle seems to run,
When the brisk minor pants for twenty-one,'"

said Mr. Walsingham, smiling, as he looked at young Beaumont. "But I think it is the mixture of fear with hope that makes time appear to pass slowly."

"And is hope ever free from that mixture?" said Miss Walsingham. "Does not hope without fear become certainty, and fear without hope despair? Can hope ever be perfectly free from some mixture of fear?"

"Oh, dear me! yes, to be sure," said Miss Hunter; "for hope's the most opposite thing that ever was to fear; as different as black and white; for, surely, every body knows that hope is just the contrary to fear; and when one says, I hope, one does not ever mean I fear—surely, you know, Mrs. Beaumont?"

"I am the worst metaphysician in the world," said Mrs. Beaumont; "I have not head enough to analyze my heart."

"Nor I neither," said Miss Hunter: "Heigho!" (very audibly.)

"Hark!" cried Mr. Beaumont, "I think I hear a horse galloping. It is he! it is Walsingham!"

Out ran Beaumont, full speed, to meet his friend; whilst, with, more sober joy, Mr. Walsingham waited on the steps, where all the company assembled, Mr. Palmer foremost, with a face full of benevolent pleasure; Mrs. Beaumont congratulating every body, but nobody listening to her; luckily for her, all were too heartily occupied with their own feelings to see how ill her countenance suited her words. The sound of the galloping of the horse ceased for a minute—then recommenced; but before it could be settled whether it was coming nearer or going farther away, Mr. Beaumont returned with a note in his hand.

"Not Walsingham—only Birch—confound him!" said Mr. Beaumont, out of breath. "Confound him, what a race I took, and how disappointed I was when I saw Birch's face; and yet it is no fault of his, poor lad!"

"But why did not he come up to the house? Why did not you let us see him?" said Mr. Walsingham.

"I could not keep him, he was in such a hurry to go home to his father and mother, he would only stop to give this note."

"From Walsingham? Read, quick."

"Plymouth, 5 o'clock, A.M. just landed.

"Dear friends, I cannot have the pleasure of seeing you, as I had hoped to do, this day—I am obliged to go to London instantly on business that must not be delayed—Cannot tell when I can be with you—hope in a few days—Well and happy, and ever yours, H. WALSINGHAM."

All stood silent with looks of disappointment, except Mrs. Beaumont, who reiterated, "What a pity! What a sad pity! What a disappointment! What a terrible disappointment!"

"Business!" said Mr. Beaumont: "curse his business! he should think of his friends first."

"Most likely his business is for his friends," said Miss Walsingham.

"That's right, my dear little defender of the absent," said Mr. Walsingham.

"Business!" repeated Mr. Palmer. "Hum! I like business better than pleasure—I will be patient, if it is really business that keeps him away from us."

"Depend upon it," said Miss Walsingham, "nothing but business can keep him away from us; his pleasure is always at home."

"I am thinking," said Mr. Palmer, drawing Mr. Walsingham aside, "I am thinking whether he has really brought this Spanish lady home with him, and what will become of her—of—him, I mean. I wish I was not going to Jamaica!"

"Then, my dear sir, where is the necessity of your going?"

"My health—my health—the physicians say I cannot live in England."

Mr. Walsingham, who had but little faith in physicians, laughed, and exclaimed, "But, my dear sir, when you see so many men alive in England at this instant, why should you believe in the impossibility of your living even in this pestiferous country?"

Mr. Palmer half smiled, felt for his snuff-box, and then replied, "I am sure I should like to live in England, if my health would let me; but," continued he, his face growing longer, and taking the hypochondriac cast as he pronounced the word, "but, Mr. Walsingham, you don't consider that my health is really—really—"

"Really very good, I see," interrupted Mr. Walsingham, "and I am heartily glad to see it."

"Sir! sir! you do not see it, I assure you. I have a great opinion of your judgment, but as you are not a physician—"

"And because I have not taken out my diploma, you think I can neither see nor understand," interrupted Mr. Walsingham. "But, nevertheless, give me leave to feel your pulse."

"Do you really understand a pulse?" said Mr. Palmer, baring his wrist, and sighing.

"As good a pulse as ever man had," pronounced Mr. Walsingham.

"You don't say so? why the physicians tell me—"

"Never mind what they tell you—if they told you the truth, they'd tell you they want fees."

Mrs. Beaumont, quite startled by the tremendously loud voice in which Mr. Walsingham pronounced the word truth, rose, and rang the bell for her carriage.

"Mr. Palmer," said she, "I am afraid we must run away, for I dread the night air for invalids."

"My good madam, I am at your orders," answered Mr. Palmer, buttoning himself up to the chin.

"Mrs. Beaumont, surely you don't think this gentleman an invalid?" said Mr. Walsingham.

"I only wish he would not think himself such," replied Mrs. Beaumont.

"Ah! my dear friends," said Mr. Palmer, "I really am, I certainly am a sad—sad—"

"Hypochondriac," said Mr. Walsingham. "Pardon me—you are indeed, and every body is afraid to tell you so but myself."

Mrs. Beaumont anxiously looked out of the window to see if her carriage was come to the door.

"Hypochondriac! not in the least, my dear sir," said Mr. Palmer. "If you were to hear what Dr. — and Dr. — say of my case, and your own Dr. Wheeler here, who has a great reputation too—shall I tell you what he says?"

In a low voice, Mr. Palmer, holding Mr. Walsingham by the button, proceeded to recapitulate some of Dr. Wheeler's prognostics; and at every pause, Mr. Walsingham turned impatiently, so as almost to twist off the detaining button, repeating, in the words of the king of Prussia to his physician, "C'est un âne! C'est un âne! C'est un âne!"—"Pshaw! I don't understand French," cried Mr. Palmer, angrily. His warmth obliged him to think of unbuttoning his coat, which operation (after stretching his neckcloth to remove an uneasy feeling in his throat) he was commencing, when Mrs. Beaumont graciously stopped his hand.

"The carriage is at the door, my dear sir:—instead of unbuttoning your coat, had not you better put this cambric handkerchief round your throat before we go into the cold air?"

Mr. Palmer put it on, as if in defiance of Mr. Walsingham, and followed Mrs. Beaumont, who led him off in triumph. Before he reached the carriage-door, however, his anger had spent its harmless force; and stopping to shake hands with him, Mr. Palmer said, "My good Mr. Walsingham, I am obliged to you. I am sure you wish me well, and I thank you for speaking so freely; I love honest friends—but as to my being a hypochondriac, believe me, you are mistaken!"

"And as to Dr. Wheeler," said Mrs. Beaumont, as she drew up the glass of the carriage, and as they drove from the door, "Dr. Wheeler certainly does not deserve to be called un âne, for he is a man of whose medical judgment I have the highest opinion. Though I am sure I am very candid to acknowledge it in the present case, when his opinion is so much against my wishes, and all our wishes, and must, I fear, deprive us so soon of the company of our dear Mr. Palmer."

"Why, yes, I must go, I must go to Jamaica," said Mr. Palmer in a more determined tone than he had yet spoken on the subject.

Mrs. Beaumont silently rejoiced; and as her son imprudently went on arguing in favour of his own wishes, she leaned back in the carriage, and gave herself up to a pleasing reverie, in which she anticipated the successful completion of all her schemes. Relieved from the apprehension that Captain Walsingham's arrival might disconcert her projects, she was now still further re-assured by Mr. Palmer's resolution to sail immediately. One day more, and she was safe. Let Mr. Palmer but sail without seeing Captain Walsingham, and this was all Mrs. Beaumont asked of fortune; the rest her own genius would obtain. She was so absorbed in thought, that she did not know she was come home, till the carriage stopped at her door. Sometimes, indeed, her reverie had been interrupted by Mr. Palmer's praises of the Walsinghams, and by a conversation which she heard going on about Captain Walsingham's life and adventures: but Captain Walsingham was safe in London; and whilst he was at that distance, she could bear to hear his eulogium. Having lamented that she had been deprived of her dear Amelia all this day, and having arranged her plan of operations for the morrow, Mrs. Beaumont retired to rest. And even in dreams her genius invented fresh expedients, wrote notes of apology, or made speeches of circumvention.

CHAPTER XI

"And now, as oft in some distempered state,
On one nice trick depends the general fate."
—POPE.

That old politician, the cardinal of Lorraine, used to say, that "a lie believed but for one hour doth many times in a nation produce effects of seven years' continuance." At this rate what wonderful effects might our heroine have produced, had she practised in public life, instead of confining her genius to family politics! The game seemed now in her own hands. The day, the important day, on which all her accounts with her son were to be settled; the day when Mr. Palmer's will was to be signed, the last day he was to stay in England, arrived. Mr. Beaumont's birthday, his coming of age, was of course hailed with every possible demonstration of joy. The village bells rang, the tenants were invited to a dinner and a dance, and an ox was to be roasted whole; and the preparations for rejoicing were heard all over the house. Mr. Palmer's benevolent heart was ever ready to take a share in the pleasures of his fellow-creatures, especially in the festivities of the lower classes. He appeared this morning in high good humour. Mrs. Beaumont, with a smile on her lips, yet with a brow of care, was considering how she could make pleasure subservient to interest, and how she could get business done in the midst of the amusements of the day. Most auspiciously did her day of business begin by Mr. Palmer's declaring to her that his will was actually made; that with the exception of certain legacies, he had left his whole fortune to her during her life, with remainder to her son and daughter. "By this arrangement," continued he, "I trust I shall ultimately serve my good friends the Walsinghams, as I wish: for though I have not seen as much of that family as I should have been glad to have done, yet the little I have seen convinces me that they are worthy people."

"The most worthy people upon earth. You know I have the greatest regard for them," said Mrs. Beaumont.

"I am really sorry," pursued Mr. Palmer, "that I have not been able to make acquaintance with Captain Walsingham. Mr. Walsingham told me his whole history yesterday, and it has prepossessed me much in his favour."

"He is, indeed, a charming, noble-hearted young hero," said Mrs. Beaumont; "and I regret, as much as you do, that you cannot see him before you leave England."

"However," continued Mr. Palmer, "as I was saying, the Walsinghams will, I trust, be the better sooner or later by me; for I think I foresee that Captain Walsingham, if a certain Spanish lady were out of the question, would propose for Amelia, and would persuade her to give up this foolish fancy of hers for that baronet."

Mrs. Beaumont shook her head, as if she believed this could not possibly be done.

"Well, well, if it can't be, it can't. The girl's inclination must not be controlled. I don't wonder, however, that you are vexed at missing such a husband for her as young Walsingham. But, my good madam, we must make the best of it—let the girl marry her baronet. I have left a legacy of some thousands to Captain Walsingham, as a token of my esteem for his character; and I am sure, my dear Mrs. Beaumont, his interests are in good hands when I leave them in yours. In the mean time, I wish you, as the representative of my late good friend, Colonel Beaumont, to enjoy all I have during your life."

Mrs. Beaumont poured forth such a profusion of kind and grateful expressions, that Mr. Palmer was quite disconcerted. "No more of this, my dear madam, no more of this. But there was something I was going to say, that has gone out of my head. Oh, it was, that the Walsinghams will, I think, stand a good chance of being the better for me in another way."

"How?"

"Why you have seen so much more of them than I have—don't you, my dear madam, see that Miss Walsingham has made a conquest of your son? I thought I was remarkably slow at seeing these things, and yet I saw it."

"Miss Walsingham is a prodigious favourite of mine. But you know Edward is so young, and men don't like, now-a-days, to marry young," said Mrs. Beaumont.

"Well, let them manage their affairs their own way," said Mr. Palmer; "all I wish upon earth is to see them happy, or rather to hear of their happiness, for I shall not see it you know in Jamaica."

"Alas!" said Mrs. Beaumont, in a most affectionate tone, and with a sigh that seemed to come from her heart; "alas! that is such a melancholy thought."

Mr. Palmer ended the conversation by inquiring whom he had best ask to witness his will. Mrs. Beaumont proposed Captain Lightbody and Dr. Wheeler. The doctor was luckily in the house, for he had been sent for this morning, to see her poor Amelia, who had caught cold yesterday, and had a slight feverish complaint.

This was perfectly true. The anxiety that Amelia had suffered of late—the fear of being forced or ensnared to marry a man she disliked—apprehensions about the Spanish incognita, and at last the certainty that Captain Walsingham would not arrive before Mr. Palmer should have left England, and that consequently the hopes she had formed from this benevolent friend's interference were vain—all these things had overpowered Amelia; she had passed a feverish night, and was really ill. Mrs. Beaumont at any other time would have been much alarmed; for, duplicity out of the question, she was a fond mother: but she now was well contented that her daughter should have a day's confinement to her room, for the sake of keeping her safe out of the way. So leaving poor Amelia to her feverish thoughts, we proceed with the business of the day.

Dr. Wheeler, Captain Lightbody, and Mr. Twigg witnessed the will; it was executed, and a copy of it deposited with Mrs. Beaumont. This was one great point gained. The next object was her jointure. She had employed her convenient tame man3, Captain Lightbody, humbly to suggest to her son, that some increase of jointure would be proper; and she was now in anxiety to know how these hints, and others which had been made by more remote means, would operate. As she was waiting to see Mr. Lightbody in her dressing-room, to hear the result of his suggestions, the door opened.

"Well, Lightbody! come in—what success?"

She stopped short, for it was not Captain Lightbody, it was her son. Without taking any notice of what she said, he advanced towards her, and presented a deed.

"You will do me the favour, mother, to accept of this addition to your jointure," said he. "It was always my intention to do this, the moment it should be in my power; and I had flattered myself that you would not have thought it necessary to suggest to me what I knew I ought to do, or to hint to me your wishes by any intermediate person."

Colouring deeply, for it hurt her conscience to be found out, Mrs. Beaumont was upon the point of disavowing her emissary, but she recollected that the words which she had used when her son was coming into the room might have betrayed her. On the other hand, it was not certain that he had heard them. She hesitated. From the shame of a disavowal, which would have answered no purpose, but to sink her lower in her son's opinion, she was, however, saved by his abrupt sincerity.

"Don't say any thing more about it, dear mother," cried he, "but pardon me the pain I have given you at a time when indeed I wished only to give pleasure. Promise me, that in future you will let me know your wishes directly, and from your own lips."

"Undoubtedly—depend upon it, my dearest son. I am quite overpowered. The fact was, that I could not, however really and urgently necessary it was to me, bring myself to mention with my own lips what, as a direct request from me, I knew you could not and would not refuse, however inconvenient it might be to you to comply. On this account, and on this account only, I wished you not to know my wants from myself, but from an intermediate friend."

"Friend!"—Mr. Beaumont could not help repeating with an emphasis of disdain.

"Friend, I only said by courtesy; but I wished you to know my wants from an intermediate person, that you might not feel yourself in any way bound, or called upon, and that the refusal might be implied and tacit, as it were, so that it could lead to no unpleasant feelings between us."

"Ah! my dear mother," said Mr. Beaumont, "I have not your knowledge of the world, or of human nature; but from all I have heard, seen, and felt, I am convinced that more unpleasant feelings are created in families, by these false delicacies, and managements, and hints, and go-between friends by courtesy, than ever would have been caused by the parties speaking directly to one another, and telling the plain truth about their thoughts and wishes. Forgive me if I speak too plainly at this moment; as we are to live together, I hope, many years, it may spare us many an unhappy hour."

Mrs. Beaumont wiped her eyes. Her son found it difficult to go on, and yet, upon his own principles, it was right to proceed.

"Amelia, ma'am! I find she is ill this morning."

"Yes—poor child!"

"I hope, mother—"

"Since," interrupted Mrs. Beaumont, "my dear son wishes always to hear from me the plain and direct truth, I must tell him, that, as the guardian of his sister, I think myself accountable to no one for my conduct with respect to her; and that I should look upon any interference as an unkind and unjustifiable doubt of my affection for my daughter. Rest satisfied with this assurance, that her happiness is, in all I do, my first object; and as I have told her a thousand times, no force shall be put on her inclinations."

"I have no more to say, no more to ask," said Mr. Beaumont. "This is a distinct, positive declaration, in which I will confide, and, in future, not suffer appearances to alarm me. A mother would not keep the word of promise to the ear, and break it to the hope."

Mrs. Beaumont, feeling herself change countenance, made an attempt to blow her nose, and succeeded in hiding her face with her handkerchief.

"With respect to myself," continued Mr. Beaumont, "I should also say, lest you should be in any doubt concerning my sentiments, that though I have complied with your request to delay for a few weeks—"

"That you need not repeat, my dear," interrupted Mrs. Beaumont. "I understand all that perfectly."

"Then at the end of this month I shall—and, I hope, with your entire approbation, propose for Miss Walsingham."

"Time enough," said Mrs. Beaumont, smiling, and tapping her son playfully on the shoulder, "time enough to talk of that when the end of the month comes. How often have I seen young men like you change their minds, and fall in and out of love in the course of one short month! At any rate," continued Mrs. Beaumont, "let us pass to the order of the day; for we have time enough to settle other matters; but the order of the day—a tiresome one, I confess—is to settle accounts."

"I am ready—"

"So am I."

"Then let us go with the accounts to Mr. Palmer, who is also ready, I am sure."

"But, before we go," said Mrs. Beaumont, whispering, "let us settle what is to be said about the debts—your debts you know. I fancy you'll agree with me, that the less is said about this the better; and that, in short, the best will be to say nothing."

"Why so, madam? Surely you don't think I mean to conceal my debts from our friend Mr. Palmer, at the very moment when I profess to tell him all my affairs, and to settle accounts with him and you, as my guardians!"

"With him? But he has never acted, you know, as one of the guardians; therefore you are not called upon to settle accounts with him."

"Then why, ma'am, did you urge him to come down from London, to be present at the settlement of these accounts?"

"As a compliment, and because I wish him to be present, as your father's friend; but it is by no means essential that he should know every detail."

"I will do whichever you please, ma'am; I will either settle accounts with or without him."

"Oh! with him, that is, in his presence, to be sure."

"Then he must know the whole."

"Why so? Your having contracted such debts will alter his opinion of your prudence and of mine, and may, perhaps, essentially alter—alter—"

"His will? Be it so; that is the worst that can happen. As far as I am concerned, I would rather a thousand times it were so, than deceive him into a better opinion of me than I deserve."

"Nobly said! so like yourself, and like every thing I could wish: but, forgive me, if I did for you, what indeed I would not wish you to do for yourself. I have already told Mr. Palmer that you had no embarrassments; therefore, you cannot, and I am sure would not, unsay what I have said."

Mr. Beaumont stood fixed in astonishment.

"But why, mother, did not you tell him the whole?"

"My dear love, delicacy prevented me. He offered to relieve you from any embarrassments, if you had any; but I, having too much delicacy and pride to let my son put himself under pecuniary obligations, hastily answered, that you had no debts; for there was no other reply to be made, without offending poor Palmer, and hurting his generous feelings, which I would not do for the universe: and I considered too, that as all Palmer's fortune will come to us in the end—"

"Well, ma'am," interrupted Mr. Beaumont, impatient of all these glosses and excuses, "the plain state of the case is, that I cannot contradict what my mother has said; therefore I will not settle accounts at all with Mr. Palmer."

"And what excuse can I make to him, after sending for him express from London?"

"That I must leave to you, mother."

"And what reason can I give for thus withdrawing our family-confidence from such an old friend, and at the very moment when he is doing so much for us all?"

"That I must leave to you, mother. I withdraw no confidence. I have pretended none—I will break none."

"Good Heavens! was not all I did and said for your interest?"

"Nothing can be for my interest that is not for my honour, and for yours, mother. But let us never go over the business again. Now to the order of the day."

"My dear, dear son," said Mrs. Beaumont, "don't speak so roughly, so cruelly to me."

Suddenly softened, by seeing the tears standing in his mother's eyes, he besought her pardon for the bluntness of his manner, and expressed his entire belief in her affection and zeal for his interests; but, on the main point, that he would not deceive Mr. Palmer, or directly or indirectly assert a falsehood, Mr. Beaumont was immoveable. In the midst of her entreaties a message came from Mr. Palmer, to say that he was waiting for the accounts, which Mrs. Beaumont wished to settle. "Well," said she, much perplexed, "well, come down to him—come, for it is impossible for me to find any excuse after sending for him from London; he would think there was something worse than there really is. Stay—I'll go down first, and sound him; and if it won't do without the accounts, do you come when I ring the bell; then all I have for it is to run my chance. Perhaps he may never recollect what passed about your debts, for the dear good old soul has not the best memory in the world; and if he should obstinately remember, why, after all, it's only a bit of false delicacy, and a white lie for a friend and a son, and we can colour it."

Down went Mrs. Beaumont to sound Mr. Palmer; but though much might be expected from her address, yet she found it unequal to the task of convincing this gentleman's plain good sense that it would fatigue him to see those accounts, which he came so many miles on purpose to settle. Perceiving him begin to waken to the suspicion that she had some interest in suppressing the accounts, and hearing him, in an altered tone, ask, "Madam, is there any mystery in these accounts, that I must not see them?" she instantly rang the bell, and answered, "Oh, none; none in the world; only we thought— that is, I feared it might fatigue you too much, my dear friend, just the day before your journey, and I was unwilling to lose so many hours of your good company; but since you are so very kind—here's my son and the papers."

CHAPTER XII

"A face untaught to feign; a judging eye,
That darts severe upon a rising lie,
And strikes a blush through frontless flattery."

To the settlement of accounts they sat down in due form; and it so happened, that though this dear good old soul had not the best memory in the world, yet he had an obstinate recollection of every word Mrs. Beaumont had said about her son's having no debts or embarrassments. And great and unmanageable was his astonishment, when the truth came to light. "It is not," said he, turning to Mr. Beaumont, "that I am astonished at your having debts; I am sorry for that, to be sure; but young men are often a little extravagant or so, and I dare say—particularly as you are so candid and make no excuses about it—I dare say you will be more prudent in future, and give up the race-horses as you promise. But—why did not Madam Beaumont tell me the truth? Why make a mystery, when I wanted nothing but to serve my friends? It was not using me well—it was not using yourself well. Madam, madam, I am vexed to the heart, and would not for a thousand pounds—ay, fool as I am, not for ten thousand pounds, this had happened to me from my good friend the colonel's widow—a man that would as soon have cut his hand off. Oh, madam! Madam Beaumont! you have struck me a hard blow at my time of life. Any thing but this I could have borne; but to have one's confidence and old friendships shaken at my time of life!"

Mrs. Beaumont was, in her turn, in unfeigned astonishment; for Mr. Palmer took the matter more seriously, and seemed more hurt by this discovery of a trifling deviation from truth, than she had foreseen, or than she could have conceived to be possible, in a case where neither his interest nor any one of his passions was concerned. It was in vain that she palliated and explained, and talked of delicacy, and generosity, and pride, and maternal feelings, and the feelings of a friend, and all manner of fine and double-refined sentiments; still Mr. Palmer's sturdy plain sense could not be made to comprehend that a falsehood is not a falsehood, or that deceiving a friend is using him well. Her son suffered for her, as his countenance and his painful and abashed silence plainly showed.

"And does not even my son say any thing for me? Is this friendly?" said she, unable to enter into his feelings, and thinking that the part of a friend was to make apologies, right or wrong.—Mr. Palmer shook hands with Mr. Beaumont, and, without uttering a syllable, they understood one another perfectly. Mr. Beaumont left the room; and Mrs. Beaumont burst into tears. Mr. Palmer, with great good-nature, tried to assuage that shame and compunction which he imagined that she felt. He observed, that, to be sure, she must feel mortified and vexed with herself, but that he was persuaded nothing but some mistaken notion of delicacy could have led her to do what her principles must condemn. Immediately she said all that she saw would please Mr. Palmer; and following the lead of his mind, she at last confirmed him in the opinion, that this was an accidental not an habitual deviation from truth. His confidence in her was broken, but not utterly destroyed.

"As to the debt," resumed Mr. Palmer, "do not let that give you a moment's concern; I will put that out of the question in a few minutes. My share in the cargo of the Anne, which I see is just safely arrived in the Downs, will more than pay this debt. Your son shall enter upon his estate unencumbered. No, no—don't thank me; I won't cheat you of your thanks; it is your son must thank me for this. I do it on his account. I like the young man. There is an ingenuousness, an honourable frankness about him, that I love. Instead of his bond for the money, I shall ask his promise never to have any thing more to do with race-horses or Newmarket; and his promise I shall think as good as if it were his bond. Now I am not throwing money away; I'm not doing an idle ostentatious thing, but one that may, and I hope will, be essentially useful. For, look you here, my good—look here, Mrs. Beaumont: a youth who finds himself encumbered with debt on coming to his estate is apt to think of freeing himself by marrying a fortune instead of a woman; now instead of freeing a man, this fetters him for life: and what sort of a friend must that be, who, if he could prevent it, would let this be done for a few thousand pounds? So I'll go before I take another pinch of snuff, and draw him an order upon the cargo of the Anne, lest I should forget it in the hurry of packing and taking leave, and all those uncomfortable things."

He left Madam Beaumont to her feelings, or her reflections; and, in a few minutes, with an order for the money in his hand, went over the house in search of his young friend. Mr. Beaumont came out of his sister's room on hearing himself called.

"Here," said Mr. Palmer, "is a little business for you to do. Read this order over; see that it is right, and endorse it—mind—and never let me hear one word more about it—only by way of acknowledgment— ask your mother what you are to give me. But don't read it till you are out of my sight—Is Amelia up? Can I see her?"

"Yes; up and in her dressing-room. Do, dear sir, go in and see her, for my mother says she is too feverish to leave her room to-day; but I am sure that it will make her ten times worse to be prevented from seeing you the last day you are with us."

"Does the little gipsy then care so much for me?—that's fair; for I am her friend, and will prove it to her, by giving up my own fancies to hers: so trust me with her, tête-à-tête,—young gentleman; go off, if you please, and do your own business."

Mr. Palmer knocked at Amelia's door, and fancying he heard an answer of admittance, went in.

"Oh, Mr. Palmer, my good Mr. Palmer, is it you?"

"Yes; but you seem not above half to know whether you are glad or sorry to see your good Mr. Palmer; for while you hold out your hand, you turn away your face from me.—Dear, dear! what a burning hand, and how the pulse goes and flutters! What does Dr. Wheeler say to this? I am a bit of a physician myself—let me look at you. What's this? eyes as red as ferret's—begging your eyes' pardon, young lady—What's this about? Come," said he, drawing a chair and sitting down close beside her, "no mysteries—no mysteries—I hate mysteries—besides, we have not time for them. Consider, I go to-morrow, and have all my shirts to pack up: ay, smile, lady, as your father used to do; and open your whole heart to me, as he always did. Consider me as an old friend."

"I do consider you as a sincere, excellent friend," said Amelia; "but—" Amelia knew that she could not explain herself without disobeying, and perhaps betraying, her mother.

"No buts," said Mr. Palmer, taking hold of her hand. "Come, my little Amelia, before you have put that ring on and off your pretty finger fifty times more, tell me whom you would wish to put a ring on this finger for life?"

"Ah! that is the thing I cannot tell you!" said Amelia. "Were I alone concerned, I would tell you every thing; but—ask me no more, I cannot tell you the whole truth."

"Then there's something wrong somewhere or other. Whenever people tell me they cannot speak the truth, I always say, then there's something wrong. Give me leave, Amelia, to ask—"

"Don't question me," said Amelia: "talk to my mother. I don't know how I ought to answer you."

"Not know how! 'Fore George! this is strange! A strange house, where one can't get at the simplest truth without a world of difficulty—mother and daughter all alike; not one of 'em but the son can, for the soul of 'em, give a plain answer to a plain question. Not know how! as if it was a science to tell the truth. Not know how! as if a person could not talk to me, honest old Richard Palmer, without knowing how! as if it was how to baffle a lawyer on a cross-examination—Not know how to answer one's own friend! Ah! this is not the way your father and I used to go on, Miss Beaumont. Nay, nay, don't cry now, or that will finish oversetting the little temper I have left, for I can't bear to see a woman cry, especially a young woman like you; it breaks my heart, old as it is, and fool that I am, that ought to know your sex better by this time than to let a few tears drown my common sense. Well, young lady, be that as it may, since you won't tell me your mind, I must tell you your mind, for I happen to know it—Yes, I do—your mother bid me spare your delicacy, and I would, but that I have not time; besides, I don't understand, nor see what good is got, but a great deal of mischief, by these cursed new-fashioned delicacies: wherefore, in plain English, I tell you, I don't like Sir John Hunter, and I do like Captain Walsingham; and I did wish you married to Captain Walsingham—you need not start so, for I say did—I don't wish it now; for since your heart is set upon Sir John Hunter, God forbid I should want to give Captain Walsingham a wife without a heart. So I have only to add, that notwithstanding my own fancy or judgment, I have done my best to persuade your mother to let you have the man, or the baronet, of your choice. I will go farther: I'll make it a point with her, and bring you both together; for there's no other way, I see, of understanding you; and get a promise of her consent; and then I hope I shall leave you all satisfied, and without any mysteries. And, in the mean time," added Mr. Palmer, taking out of his coat pocket a morocco leather case, and throwing it down on the table before Amelia, "every body should be made happy their own way: there are some diamonds for Lady Hunter, and God bless you."

"Oh, sir, stay!" cried Amelia, rising eagerly; "dear, good Mr. Palmer, keep your diamonds, and leave me your esteem and love."

"That I can't, unless you speak openly to me. It is out of nature. Don't kneel—don't. God bless you! young lady, you have my pity; for indeed," turning and looking at her, "you seem very miserable, and look very sincere."

"If my mother was here!—I must see my mother," exclaimed Amelia.

"Where's the difficulty? I'll go for her this instant," said Mr. Palmer, who was not a man to let a romance trail on to six volumes for want of going six yards; or for want of somebody's coming into a room at the right minute for explanation; or from some of those trivial causes by which adepts contrive to delude us at the very moment of expectation. Whilst Mr. Palmer was going for Mrs. Beaumont, Amelia waited in terrible anxiety. The door was open; and as she looked into the gallery which led to her room, she saw Mr. Palmer and her mother as they came along, talking together. Knowing every symptom of suppressed passion in her mother's countenance, she was quite terrified, by indications which passed unnoticed by Mr. Palmer. As her mother approached, Amelia hid her face in her hands for a moment, but gaining courage from the consciousness of integrity, and from a determination to act openly, she looked up; and, rising with dignity, said, in a gentle but firm voice—"Mother, I hope you will not think that there is any impropriety in my speaking to our friend, Mr. Palmer, with the same openness with which I have always spoken to you?"

"My dear child," interrupted Mrs. Beaumont, embracing Amelia with a sudden change of manner and countenance, "my sweet child, I have tried you to the utmost; forgive me; all your trials now are over, and you must allow me the pleasure of telling our excellent friend, Mr. Palmer, what I know will delight him almost as much as it delights me—that the choice of Amelia's heart, Mr. Palmer, is worthy of her, just what we all wished."

"Captain Walsingham?" exclaimed Mr. Palmer, with joyful astonishment.

"Sit down, my love," said Mrs. Beaumont, seating Amelia, who, from the surprise at this sudden change in her mother, and from the confusion of feelings which overwhelmed her at this moment, was near fainting: "we are too much for her, I have been too abrupt," continued Mrs. Beaumont: "Open the window, will you, my good sir? and," whispering, "let us not say any more to her at present; you see it won't do."

"I am well, quite well again, now," said Amelia, exerting herself. "Don't leave, don't forsake me, Mr. Palmer; pray don't go," holding out her hand to Mr. Palmer.

"My dear Amelia," said Mrs. Beaumont, "don't talk, don't exert yourself; pray lie still on the sofa."

"Her colour is come back; she looks like herself again," said Mr. Palmer, seating himself beside her, regardless of Mrs. Beaumont's prohibitory looks. "Since my little Amelia wished me to stay, I'll not go. So, my child—but I won't hurry you—only want one sign of the head to confirm the truth of what your mother has just told me, for nobody can tell what passes in a young lady's heart but herself. So then, it is not that sprig of quality, that selfish spendthrift, that Sir John Hunter, who has your heart—hey?"

"No, no, no," answered Amelia; "I never did, I never could like such a man!"

"Why, I thought not—I thought it was impossible; but—"

Mrs. Beaumont, alarmed beyond conception, suddenly put her hand before Mr. Palmer's mouth, to prevent him from finishing his sentence, and exposing the whole of her shameful duplicity to her daughter.

"Absolutely I must, and do hereby interpose my maternal authority, and forbid all agitating explanations whilst Amelia is in her present state. Dr. Wheeler says she is terribly feverish. Come, Mr. Palmer, I must carry you off by force, and from me you shall have all the explanations and all the satisfaction you can require."

"Well," said Mr. Palmer, "good bye for the present, my little Amelia, my darling little Amelia! I am so delighted to find that Captain Walsingham's the man, and so glad you have no mysteries: be well, be well soon. I am so pleased, so happy, that I am as unruly as a child, and as easily managed. You see, how I let myself be turned out of the room."

"Not turned out, only carried out," said Mrs. Beaumont, who never, even in the most imminent perils, lost her polite presence of mind. Having thus carried off Mr. Palmer, she was in hopes that, in the joyful confusion of his mind, he would he easily satisfied with any plausible explanation. Therefore she dexterously fixed his attention on the future, and adverted as slightly as possible to the past.

"Now, my good sir, congratulate me," said she, "on the prospect I have of happiness in such a son-in-law as Captain Walsingham, if it be indeed true that Captain Walsingham is really attached to Amelia. But, on the other hand, what shall we do if there is any truth in the story of the Spanish lady? Oh, there's the difficulty! Between hope and fear, I am in such a distracted state at this moment, I hardly know what I say. What shall we do about the Spanish lady?"

"Do, my dear madam! we can do nothing at all in that case: but I will hope the best, and you'll see that he will prove a constant man at last. In the mean time, how was all that about Sir John Hunter, and what are you to do with him?"

"Leave that to me; I will settle all that," cried Mrs. Beaumont.

"But I hope the poor man, though I don't like him, has not been jilted?"

"No, by no means; Amelia's incapable of that. You know she told you just now that she never liked him."

"Ay; but I think, madam, you told me, that she did," said Mr. Palmer, sticking to his point with a decided plainness, which quite disconcerted Mrs. Beaumont.

"It was all a mistake," said she, "quite a mistake; and I am sure you rejoice with me that it was so: and, as to the rest—past blunders, like past misfortunes, are good for nothing but to be forgotten."

Observing that Mr. Palmer looked dissatisfied, Mrs. Beaumont continued apologizing. "I confess you have to all appearance some cause to be angry with me," said she: "but now only hear me. Taking the blame upon myself, let me candidly tell you the whole truth, and all my reasons, foolish perhaps as they were. Captain Walsingham behaved so honourably, and had such command over his feelings, that I, who am really the most credulous creature in the world, was so completely deceived, that I fancied he never had a thought of Amelia, and that he never would think of her; and I own this roused both my pride and my prudence for my daughter; and I certainly thought it my duty, as her mother, to do every thing in my power to discourage in her young and innocent heart a hopeless passion. It was but within these few hours that I have been undeceived by you as to his sentiments. That, of course, made an immediate change, as you have seen, in my measures; for such is my high opinion of the young man, and indeed my desire to be connected with the Walsinghams is so great, that even whilst I am in total ignorance of what the amount or value may be of this prize that he has taken, and even whilst I am in doubt concerning this Spanish incognita, I have not hesitated to declare, perhaps imprudently, to Amelia, as you have just heard, my full approbation of the choice of her heart."

"Hum!—well—hey!—How's this?" said Mr. Palmer to himself, as he tried to believe and to be satisfied with this apology. "Madam," said he aloud to Mrs. Beaumont, "I comprehend that it might not be prudent to encourage Amelia's partiality for Captain Walsingham till you were sure of the young man's sentiments; but, excuse me, I am a very slow, unpractised man in these matters; I don't yet understand why you told me that she was in love with Sir John Hunter?"

Mrs. Beaumont, being somewhat in the habit of self-contradiction, was seldom unprovided with a concordance of excuses; but at this unlucky moment she was found unprepared. Hesitating she stood, all subtle as she was, deprived of ready wit, and actually abashed in the presence of a plain good man.

"I candidly confess, my dear sir," said she, apologizing to Mr. Palmer as he walked up and down, "that my delicacy or pride,—call it what you will,—my false pride for my daughter, led me into an error. I could not bring myself to acknowledge to any man, even to you—for you know that it's contrary quite to the principles and pride of our sex—that she felt any partiality for a man who had shown none for her.

You must be sensible it was, to say no more, an awkward, mortifying thing; and I was so afraid even of your finding it out, that—forgive me—I did, I candidly acknowledge, fabricate the foolish story of Sir John Hunter. But, believe me, I never seriously thought of her marrying him."

"'Fore George! I don't understand one word of it from beginning to end," said Mr. Palmer, speaking aloud to himself.

Regardless of the profusion of words which Mrs. Beaumont continued pouring forth, he seated himself in an arm-chair, and, deep in reverie for some minutes, went on slowly striking his hands together, as he leaned with his arms on his knees. At length he rose, rang the bell, and said to the servant, "Sir, be so obliging as to let my man Crichton know that he need not hurry himself to pack up my clothes, for I shall not go to-morrow."

Struck with consternation at these words, Mrs. Beaumont, nevertheless, commanded the proper expression of joy on the occasion. "Delightful! I must go this instant," cried she, "and be the first to tell this charming news to Amelia and Edward."

"Tell them, then, madam, if you please, that I have gained such a conquest over what Mr. Walsingham calls my hypochondriacism, that I am determined, at whatever risk, to stay another year in Old England, and that I hope to be present at both their weddings."

Mrs. Beaumont's quick exit was at this moment necessary to conceal her dismay. Instead of going to Amelia, she hurried to her own room, locked the door, and sat down to compose her feelings and to collect her thoughts; but scarcely had she been two minutes in her apartment, when a messenger came to summon her to the festive scene in the park. The tenants and villagers were all at dinner, and Mr. Beaumont sent to let her know that they were waiting to drink her health. She was obliged to go, and to appear all radiant with pleasure. The contrast between their honest mirth and her secret sufferings was great. She escaped as soon as she could from their senseless joy, and again shut herself up in her own room.

This sudden and totally unexpected resolution of Mr. Palmer's so astonished her, that she could scarcely believe she had heard or understood his words rightly. Artful persons may, perhaps, calculate with expertness and accuracy what will, in any given case, be the determinations of the selfish and the interested; but they are liable to frequent mistakes in judging of the open-hearted and the generous: there is no sympathy to guide them, and all their habits tend to mislead them in forming opinions of the direct and sincere. It had never entered into Mrs. Beaumont's imagination that Mr. Palmer would, notwithstanding his belief that he hazarded his life by so doing, defer a whole year returning to Jamaica, merely to secure the happiness of her son and daughter. She plainly saw that he now suspected her dislike to the Walsinghams, and her aversion to the double union with that family: she saw that the slightest circumstance in her conduct, which confirmed his suspicions, would not only utterly ruin her in his opinion, but might induce him to alter that part of his will which left her sole possessor of his fortune during her life. Bad as her affairs were at this moment, she knew that they might still be worse. She recollected the letter of perfect approbation which Sir John Hunter had in his power. She foresaw that he would produce this letter on the first rumour of her favouring another lover for Amelia. She had just declared to Mr. Palmer, that she never seriously thought of Sir John Hunter for her daughter; and, should this letter be brought to light, she must be irremediably convicted of the basest duplicity, and there would be no escape from the shame of falsehood, or rather the disgrace of detection. In this grand difficulty, Mrs. Beaumont was too good a politician to waste time upon any inferior considerations.

Instead of allowing herself leisure to reflect that all her present difficulties arose from her habits of insincerity, she, with the true spirit of intrigue, attributed her disappointments to some deficiency of artifice. "Oh!" said she to herself, "why did I write? I should only have spoken to Sir John. How could I be so imprudent as to commit myself by writing? But what can be done to repair this error?"

One web destroyed, she, with indefatigable subtlety, began to weave another. With that promptitude of invention which practice alone can give, she devised a scheme, by which she hoped not only to prevent Sir John Hunter from producing the written proof of her duplicity, but by which she could also secure the reversionary title, and the great Wigram estate. The nature of the scheme shall be unfolded in the next chapter; and it will doubtless procure for Mrs. Beaumont, from all proper judges, a just tribute of admiration. They will allow our heroine to be possessed not only of that address, which is the peculiar glory of female politicians, but also of that masculine quality, which the greatest, wisest, of mankind has pronounced to be the first, second, and third requisite for business—"Boldness—boldness—boldness."

CHAPTER XIII

"The creature's at her dirty work again."
—POPE.

Amongst the infinite petty points of cunning of which that great practical philosopher Bacon has in vain essayed to make out a list, he notes that, "Because it worketh better when any thing seemeth to be gotten from you by question than if you offer it of yourself: you may lay a bait for a question, by showing another visage and countenance than you are wont, to the end to give occasion to the party to ask what the matter is of the change."

"What is the matter, my dearest Mrs. Beaumont? I never saw you look so sad before in all my life," said Miss Hunter, meeting Mrs. Beaumont, who had walked out into the park on purpose to be so met, and in hopes of having the melancholy of her countenance thus observed. It was the more striking, and the more unseasonable, from its contrast with the gay scene in the park. The sound of music was heard, and the dancing had begun, and all was rural festivity: "What is the matter, my dearest Mrs. Beaumont?" repeated Miss Hunter; "at such a time as this to see you look so melancholy!"

"Ah! my love! such a sad change in affairs! But," whispered Mrs. Beaumont, "I cannot explain myself before your companion."

Mr. Lightbody was walking with Miss Hunter: but he was so complaisant, that he was easily despatched on some convenient errand; and then Mrs. Beaumont, with all her wonted delicacy of circumlocution, began to communicate her distress to her young friend.

"You know, my beloved Albina," said she, "it has been my most ardent wish that your brother should be connected with my family by the nearest and dearest ties."

"Yes; that is, married to Amelia," said Miss Hunter. "And has any thing happened to prevent it?"

"Oh, my dear! it is all over! It cannot be—must not be thought of—must not be spoken of any more; Mr. Palmer has been outrageous about it. Such a scene as I have had! and all to no purpose. Amelia has won him over to her party. Only conceive what I felt—she declared, beyond redemption, her preference of Captain Walsingham."

"Before the captain proposed for her! How odd! dear! Suppose he should never propose for her, what a way she will be in after affronting my brother and all! And only think! she gives up the title, and the great Wigram estate, and every thing. Why, my brother says, uncle Wigram can't live three months; and Lord Puckeridge's title, too, will come to my brother, you know; and Amelia might have been Lady Puckeridge. Only think! did you ever know any thing so foolish?"

"Never!" said Mrs. Beaumont; "but you know, my dear, so few girls have the sense you show in taking advice: they all will judge for themselves. But I'm most hurt by Amelia's want of gratitude and delicacy towards me," continued Mrs. Beaumont; "only conceive the difficulty and distress in which she has left me about your poor brother. Such a shock as the disappointment will be to him! And he may—though Heaven knows how little I deserve it—he may suspect—for men, when they are vexed and angry, will, you know, suspect even their best friends; he might, I say, suspect me of not being warm in his cause."

"Dear, no! I have always told him how kind you were, and how much you wished the thing; and of all people in the world he can't blame you, dearest Mrs. Beaumont."

At this instant Mrs. Beaumont saw a glimpse of somebody in a bye-path of the shrubbery near them. "Hush! Take care! Who is that lurking there? Some listener! Who can it be?"

Miss Hunter applied her glass to her eye, but could not make out who it was.

"It is Lightbody, I declare," said Mrs. Beaumont. "Softly,—let us not pretend to see him, and watch what he will do. It is of the greatest consequence to me to know whether he is a listener or not; so much as he is about the house."

An irresistible fit of giggling, which seized Miss Hunter at the odd way in which Lightbody walked, prevented Mrs. Beaumont's trial of his curiosity. At the noise which the young lady made, Mr. Lightbody turned his head, and immediately advancing, with his accustomed mixture of effrontery and servility, said, that "he had executed Mrs. Beaumont's commands, and that he had returned in hopes of getting a moment to say a word to her when she was at leisure, about something he had just learned from Mr. Palmer's man Crichton, which it was of consequence she should know without delay."

"Oh, thank you, you best of creatures; but I know all that already."

"You know that Mr. Palmer does not go to-morrow?"

"Yes; and am so rejoiced at it! Do, my dear Lightbody, go to Amelia and my son from me, and tell them that charming news. And after that, pray have the compassion to inquire if the post is not come in yet, and run over the papers, to see if you can find any thing about Walsingham's prize."

Mr. Lightbody obeyed, but not with his usual alacrity. Mrs. Beaumont mused for a moment, and then said, "I do believe he was listening. What could he be doing there?"

"Doing!—Oh, nothing," said Miss Hunter: "he's never doing any thing, you know; and as to listening, he was so far off he could not hear a word we said: besides, he is such a simple creature, and loves you so!"

"I don't know," said Mrs. Beaumont; "he either did not play me fair, or else he did a job I employed him in this morning so awkwardly, that I never wish to employ him again. He is but a low kind of person, after all; I'll get rid of him: that sort of people always grow tiresome and troublesome after a time, and one must shake them off. But I have not leisure to think of him now—Well, my dear, to go on with what I was saying to you."

Mrs. Beaumont went on talking of her friendship for Sir John Hunter, and of the difficulty of appeasing him; but observing that Miss Hunter listened only with forced attention, she paused to consider what this could mean. Habitually suspicious, like all insincere people, Mrs. Beaumont now began to imagine that there was some plot carrying on against her by Sir John Hunter and Lightbody, and that Miss Hunter was made use of against her. Having a most contemptible opinion of her Albina's understanding, and knowing that her young friend had too little capacity to be able to deceive her, or to invent a plausible excuse impromptu, Mrs. Beaumont turned quick, and exclaimed, "My dear, what could Lightbody be saying to you when I came up?—for I remember he stopped short, and you both looked so guilty."

"Guilty! did I?—Did he?—Dearest Mrs. Beaumont, don't look at me so with your piercing eyes!—Oh! I vow and protest I can't tell you; I won't tell you."

The young lady tittered, and twisted herself into various affected attitudes; then kissing Mrs. Beaumont, and then turning her back with childish playfulness, she cried, "No, I won't tell you; never, never, never!"

"Come, come, my dear, don't trifle; I have really business to do, and am in a hurry."

"Well, don't look at me—never look at me again—promise me that, and I'll tell you. Poor Lightbody— Oh, you're looking at me!—Poor Lightbody was talking to me of somebody, and he laid me a wager—but I can't tell you that—Ah, don't be angry with me, and I will tell, if you'll turn your head quite away!— that I should be married to somebody before the end of this year. Oh, now, don't look at me, dearest, dearest Mrs. Beaumont."

"You dear little simpleton, and was that all?" said Mrs. Beaumont, vexed to have wasted her time upon such folly: "come, be serious now, my dear; if you knew the anxiety I am in at this moment—" But wisely judging that it would be in vain to hope for any portion of the love-sick damsel's attention, until she had confirmed her hopes of being married to somebody before the end of the year, Mrs. Beaumont scrupled not to throw out assurances, in which she had herself no further faith. After what she had heard from her son this morning, she must have been convinced that there was no chance of marrying him to Miss Hunter; she knew indeed positively, that he would soon declare his real attachment, but she could, she thought, during the interval retain her power over Miss Hunter, and secure her services, by concealing the truth.

"Before I say one word more of my own affairs, let me, my dearest child, assure you, that in the midst of all these disappointments and mortifications about Amelia, I am supported by the hope—by something more than the hope—that I shall see the daughter of my heart happily settled soon: Lightbody does not want penetration, I see. But I am not at liberty to say more. So now, my dear, help me with all your cleverness to consider what I shall do in the difficulties I am in at this moment. Your brother has a letter of mine, approving, and so forth, his addresses to my daughter; now, if he, in the first rashness of his anger, should produce this to Palmer, I'm undone—or to my son, worse and worse! there would be a duel between them infallibly, for Beaumont is so warm on any point of honour—Oh, I dread to think of it, my dear!"

"So do I, I'm sure; but, Lord, I'm the worst person to think in a hurry—But can't you write a letter? for you always know what to say so well—And after all, do you know, I don't think he'll be half so angry or so disappointed as you fancy, for I never thought he was so much in love with Amelia."

"Indeed!"

"I know, if it was not a secret, I could tell you—"

"What? No secrets between us, my darling child."

"Then I can tell you, that just before he proposed for Amelia, he was consulting with me about proposing for Mrs. Dutton."

"Mrs. Dutton, the widow! Mrs. Dutton! How you astonish me!" said Mrs. Beaumont (though she knew this before). "Why she is older than I am."

"Older! yes, a great deal; but then you know my brother is no chicken himself."

"To be sure, compared with you, my dear, he is not young. There's a prodigious difference between you."

"Above twenty years; for, you know, he's by another marriage."

"True; but I can't believe he proposed for Mrs. Dutton."

"Not actually proposed, because I would not let him; for I should have hated to have had such an unfashionable-looking woman for my sister-in-law. I never could have borne to go into public with her, you know: so I plagued my brother out of it; and luckily he found out that her jointure is not half so great as it was said to be."

"I could have told him that. Mrs. Dutton's jointure is nothing nearly so large as mine was, even before the addition to it which my son so handsomely, and indeed unexpectedly, made to it this morning. And did I tell you, my dear? Mr. Palmer, this day, has been so kind as to leave me all his immense fortune for my own life. But don't mention it, lest it should get round, and make ill-will: the Walsinghams know nothing of it. But to return to your poor brother—if I could any way serve him with Mrs. Dutton?"

"La! he'd never think of her more—and I'm sure I would not have him."

"You dear little saucy creature! indeed I cannot wonder that you don't like the thoughts of Mrs. Dutton for a chaperon in town."

"Oh, horrid! horrid!"

"And yet, would you condemn your poor brother to be an old bachelor, after this disappointment with Amelia?"

"La, ma'am, can't he marry any body but Mrs. Dutton?"

"I wish I could think of any person would suit him. Can you?'

"Oh, I know very well who I think would suit him, and one I like to go into public with of all things."

"Who?"

"And one who has promised to present me at court next winter."

"My dearest child! is it possible that you mean me?"

"I do;—and why not?"

"Why not! My sweet love, do you consider my age?"

"But you look so young."

"To be sure Mrs. Dutton looks older, and is older; but I could not bring myself, especially after being a widow so long, to think of marrying a young man—to be sure, your brother is not what one should call a very young man."

"Dear, no; you don't look above three, or four, or five years older than he does; and in public, and with dress, and rouge, and fashion, and all that, I think it would do vastly well, and nobody would think it odd at all. There's Lady —, is not she ten years older than Lord —? and every body says that's nothing, and that she gives the most delightful parties. Oh, I declare, dearest Mrs. Beaumont, you must and shall marry my brother, and that's the only way to make him amends, and prevent mischief between the gentlemen; the only way to settle every thing charmingly—and I shall so like it—and I'm so proud of its being my plan! I vow, I'll go and write to my brother this minute, and—"

"Stay, you dear mad creature; only consider what you are about."

"Consider! I have considered, and I must and will have my own way," said the dear mad creature, struggling with Mrs. Beaumont, who detained her with an earnest hand. "My love," said she, "I positively cannot let you use my name in such a strange way. If your brother or the world should think I had any share in the transaction, it would be so indelicate."

"Indelicate! Dear me, ma'am, but when nobody will know it, how can it be indelicate? and I will not mention your name, and nobody will ever imagine that you knew any thing of my writing; and I shall manage it all my own way; and the plan is all my own: so let me go and write this minute."

"Mercy upon me! what shall I do with this dear headstrong creature!" said Mrs. Beaumont, letting Miss Hunter go, as if exhausted by the struggle she had made to detain her impetuous young friend. Away ran Miss Hunter, sometimes looking back in defiance and laughing, whilst Mrs. Beaumont shook her head at her whenever she looked back, but found it impossible to overtake her, and vain to make further opposition. As Mrs. Beaumont walked slowly homewards, she meditated her own epistle to Sir John Hunter, and arranged her future plan of operations.

If, thought she, Miss Hunter's letter should not succeed, it is only a suggestion of hers, of which I am not supposed to know any thing, and I am only just where I was before. If it does succeed, and if Sir John transfers his addresses to me, I avoid all danger of his anger on account of his disappointment with Amelia; for it must then be his play, to convince me that he is not at all disappointed, and then I shall have leisure to consider whether I shall marry Sir John or not. At all events, I can draw on his courtship as long as I please, till I have by degrees brought Mr. Palmer round to approve of the match.

With these views Mrs. Beaumont wrote an incomparable letter to Sir John Hunter, in which she enveloped her meaning in so many words, and so much sentiment, that it was scarcely possible to comprehend any thing, except, "that she should be glad to see Sir John Hunter the next day, to explain to him a circumstance that had given her, on his account, heartfelt uneasiness." Miss Hunter's letter was carefully revised by Mrs. Beaumont, though she was to know nothing of it; and such was the art with which it was retouched, that, after all proper corrections, nothing appeared but the most childish and imprudent simplicity.

After having despatched these letters, Mrs. Beaumont felt much anxiety about the effect which they might produce; but she was doomed by her own habits of insincerity to have perpetually the irksome task of assuming an appearance contrary to her real feelings. Amelia was better, and Mr. Palmer's determination to stay in England had spread a degree of cheerfulness over the whole family, which had not been felt for some time at Beaumont Park. In this general delight Mrs. Beaumont was compelled seemingly to sympathize: she performed her part so well, that even Dr. Wheeler and Captain Lightbody, who had been behind the scenes, began to believe that the actress was in earnest. Amelia, alas! knew her mother too well to be the dupe even of her most consummate powers of acting. All that Mrs. Beaumont said about her joy, and her hopes that Captain Walsingham would soon appear and confirm her happy pre-sentiments, Amelia heard without daring to believe. She had such an opinion of her mother's address, such a sublime superstitious dread that her mother would, by some inscrutable means, work out her own purposes, that she felt as if she could not escape from these secret machinations. Amelia still apprehended that Sir John Hunter would not be irrevocably dismissed, and that by some turn of artifice she should find herself bound to him. The next morning Sir John Hunter, however, finally relieved her from these apprehensions. After having been closeted for upwards of two hours with Mrs. Beaumont, he begged to speak to Miss Beaumont; and he resigned all pretensions to the honour which he had so long and so ardently aspired to. It was his pride to show that his spirits were not affected by this disappointment: he scarcely indeed exhibited that decent appearance of mortification which is usually expected on such an occasion; but with provoking haughtiness professed himself sincerely obliged to Miss Beaumont for having, however late in the business, prevented him, by her candour, from the danger of crossing her inclinations. For this he could scarcely be sufficiently thankful, when he considered how every day showed the consequences of marrying young ladies whose affections were previously engaged. He had only to add, that he hoped the world would see the thing in the same light in which he took it, and that Miss Beaumont might not find herself blamed for breaking off the matter, after it had been so publicly reported: that, for his part, he assured her, he would, as far as he was concerned, do his utmost to silence unpleasant observations; and that, as the most effectual means to do this, he conceived, would be to show that he continued on an amicable footing with the family, he should do himself the honour to avail himself of the permission—invitation, indeed—he had just received from Mrs. Beaumont, to continue his visits as usual at Beaumont Park.

To this Amelia could make no objection after the express declaration which he had just made, that he renounced all pretensions to her favour. However keenly she felt the implied reproach of having encouraged Sir John as her admirer, while her affections were previously engaged, and of having shown candour late in this affair, she could not vindicate herself without accusing her mother; therefore she attempted neither excuse nor apology, submitted to let the unfeeling baronet enjoy her confusion, whilst she said, in general terms, she felt obliged by his assurance that she should not be the cause of any quarrel between two families who had hitherto lived in friendship.

CHAPTER XIV

"Him no soft thoughts, no gratitude could move;
To gold he fled, from beauty and from love!"
DRYDEN

All that passed in the two hours' conversation between the discarded baronet and the mother of his late mistress did not transpire; but Mrs. Beaumont said that she had taken infinite pains to reconcile Sir John to his fate, and his subsequent behaviour showed that she had succeeded. His attention towards her also plainly proved that he was not dissatisfied by the part she had acted, or rather by the part that he thought she had acted. Thus all things went on smoothly. Mrs. Beaumont, in confidence, told her friend, Miss Hunter, that Sir John had behaved with the greatest propriety and candour (candour! that hackneyed word); that he had acknowledged that his principal inducement to propose for her daughter had been a desire to be connected with a family for which he had such peculiar regard.

"This, my love," continued Mrs. Beaumont, "was all, you know, that your brother could, with propriety, say on such an occasion; all indeed that I would permit him to say. As to the rest, on Amelia's account, you know, I could not refuse his request to continue his visits in this family on the same footing of friendship as usual."

Whether this was the truth and the whole truth, the mystery that involves all cabinet-councils, and more especially those of female politicians, prevents the cautious historian from presuming to decide. But arguing from general causes, and from the established characters and ruling passions of the parties concerned, we may safely conjecture that the baronet did not at this time make any decisive proposal to the lady, but that he kept himself at liberty to advance or recede, as circumstances should render it expedient. His ruling passion was avarice; and though he had been allured by the hints which his sister had thrown out concerning Mrs. Beaumont's increased jointure, and vast expectancies from Mr. Palmer, yet he was not so rash as to act decisively upon such vague information: he had wisely determined to obtain accurate and positive evidence from Captain Lightbody, who seemed, in this case, to be the common vouchee; but Lightbody happened to be gone out to shoot flappers.

Consequently Sir John wisely entrenched himself in general professions of regard to Mrs. Beaumont, and reflections on the happiness of being connected with such a respectable family. Mrs. Beaumont, who understood the whole of the game, now saw that her play must be to take Captain Lightbody again into her confidence.

Ever careful not to commit herself, she employed Miss Hunter to communicate her own scheme to the captain, and to prepare him on the requisite points with proper answers to those inquiries which she foresaw the baronet would make.

"You know, my love," said Mrs. Beaumont, "you can find a proper moment to say all you wish to Lightbody."

"Oh, yes," said Miss Hunter, "I will if I possibly can this day; but it is so difficult to find a good time—"

"At dinner, suppose?" said Mrs. Beaumont.

"At dinner! surely, ma'am, that's an awkward time, is not it, for talking of secrets?"

"The best time in the world, my dear; you know we are to have the Duttons, and the Lord knows whom besides, to-day. And when there's a large company, and every body talking at once, and eating, and drinking, and carving, it is the best time in the world! You may say what you please; your neighbours are all happily engaged, too busy to mind you. Get near fat Mr. Dutton, and behind the screen of his prodigious elbow you will be comfortably recessed from curious impertinents. My dear, the most perfect solitude is not so convenient as one of these great dinners."

Whilst Mrs. Beaumont was demonstrating to Miss Hunter that the most convenient and secure time for a tête-à-tête is at a large dinner, she happened to look out of the window, near which they were standing, and she saw her son and daughter with Mr. Palmer walking in the park; they sat down under a tree within view of the house.

"Come away from the window, my dear," said Mrs. Beaumont; "they will observe us, and perhaps think we are plotting something. I wonder what they are talking of! Look how earnestly Amelia is stretching out her neck, and Mr. Palmer striking his cane upon the ground. Come back a little, my dear, come back; you can see as well here."

"But I see a gentleman on horseback, galloping. Oh, ma'am, look! he has stopped! he has jumped off his horse! Captain Walsingham it must be!"

"Captain Walsingham it really is!" said Mrs. Beaumont, pressing forward to look out of the window, yet standing so, that she could not be seen from without.

"Dear," said Miss Hunter, "but how delighted Mr. Beaumont seems; and how Mr. Palmer shakes Captain Walsingham's hand, as if he had known him these hundred years! What can make them so glad to see him? Do look at them, ma'am."

"I see it all!" said Mrs. Beaumont, with an involuntary sigh.

"But, dear Mrs. Beaumont," pursued Miss Hunter, "if he has actually come at last to propose for Amelia, don't you think he is doing it in a shabby sort of way? When he has been in London too—and if he has taken such a treasure too, could not he have come down here a little more in style, with some sort of an equipage of his own at least? But now only look at him; would you, if you met him on the road, know him from any common man?"

Another sigh, deep and sincere, was all the answer Mrs. Beaumont made.

"I am sure," continued Miss Hunter, as Mrs. Beaumont drew her away from the window, "I am sure, I think Amelia has not gained much by the change of admirers; for what's a captain of a ship?"

"He ranks with a colonel in the army, to be sure," said Mrs. Beaumont; "but Amelia might have looked much higher. If she does not know her own interest and dignity, that is not my fault."

"If she had such a fortune as I shall have," said Miss Hunter, "she might afford to marry for love, because you know she could make her husband afterwards keep her proper equipages, and take her to town, and go into parliament, and get a title for her too!"

"Very true, my darling," said Mrs. Beaumont, who was at this instant so absent, that she assented without having heard one syllable that her darling said.

"But for Amelia, who has no such great fortune of her own, it is quite another thing, you know, dearest Mrs. Beaumont. Oh, you'll see how she'll repent when she sees you Lady Puckeridge, and herself plain Mrs. Walsingham. And when she sees the figure you'll make in town next winter, and the style my brother will live in—Oh, then she'll see what a difference there is between Sir John Hunter and Captain Walsingham!"

"Very true, indeed, my dear," said Mrs. Beaumont; and this time she did not answer without having heard the assertion. The door opened.

"Captain Walsingham! dare I believe my eyes? And do I see our friend, Captain Walsingham, again at last?"

"At last! Oh, Mrs. Beaumont, you don't know how hard I have worked to get here."

"How kind! But won't you sit down and tell me?"

"No; I can neither sit, nor rest, nor speak, nor think upon any subject but one," said Captain Walsingham.

"That's right," cried Mr. Palmer.

"Mrs. Beaumont—pardon my abruptness," continued Captain Walsingham, "but you see before you a man whose whole happiness is at stake. May I beg a few minutes' conversation with you?"

"This instant," said Mrs. Beaumont, hesitating; but she saw that Mr. Palmer's eye was upon her, so with a smile she complied immediately; and giving her hand graciously to Captain Walsingham, she accompanied him into a little reading-room within the drawing-room.

"May I hope that we are friends?" said Captain Walsingham; "may I hope so, Mrs. Beaumont—may I?"

"Good Heavens! Friends! assuredly; I hope so. I have always had and expressed the highest opinion of you, Captain Walsingham."

"I have had one, and, hitherto, but one opportunity of showing myself, in any degree, deserving of your esteem, madam," said Captain Walsingham. "When I was in this country some years ago, you must have seen how passionately I was in love with your daughter; but I knew that my circumstances were then such that I could not hope to obtain Miss Beaumont's hand; and you will do me the justice to allow that I behaved with prudence. Of the difficulty of the task I alone can judge."

Mrs. Beaumont declared, that she admired Captain Walsingham's conduct inexpressibly, now that she understood what his feelings and motives had been; but really he had kept his own secret so honourably, that she had not, till within these few days, when it was let out by Mr. Walsingham to Mr. Palmer, had the most distant idea of his being attached to her daughter.

Captain Walsingham was too polite even to look a doubt of the truth of a lady's assertion: he therefore believed, because it was impossible.

Mrs. Beaumont, determining to make her story consistent, repeated nearly what she had said to Mr. Palmer, and went on to confess that she had often, with a mother's pride, perhaps, in her own secret thoughts wondered at the indifference Captain Walsingham showed towards Amelia.

Captain Walsingham was surprised that Mrs. Beaumont's penetration should have been so strangely mistaken; especially as the symptoms of admiration and love must be so well known to a lady who had so many and such passionate admirers.

Mrs. Beaumont smiled, and observed, that Captain Walsingham, though a seaman, had all the address of a courtier, and she acknowledged that she loved address.

"If by address Mrs. Beaumont means politeness, I admire it as much as she does; but I disclaim and despise all that paltry system of artifice, which is sometimes called address. No person of a great mind ever condescends to use address in that sense of the word; not because they cannot, but because they will not."

"Certainly—certainly," said Mrs. Beaumont; "there is nothing I love so much as frankness."

"Then, frankly, Mrs. Beaumont, may I hope for your approbation in addressing Miss Beaumont?"

"Frankly, then, you have my full approbation. This is the very thing I have long secretly wished, as Mr. Palmer can tell you. You have ever been the son-in-law of my choice, though not of my hopes."

Delighted with this frank answer, this full approbation, this assurance that he had always been the son-in-law of her choice, Captain Walsingham poured out his warm heart in joy and gratitude. All suspicions of Mrs. Beaumont were forgotten; for suspicion was unnatural to his mind: though he knew, though he had experience almost from childhood, of her character, yet, at this instant, he thought he had, till now, been always prejudiced, always mistaken. Happy those who can be thus duped by the warmth of their own hearts! It is a happiness which they who smile in scorn at their credulity can never enjoy.

Wakening a little to the use of his understanding, Captain Walsingham disconcerted Mrs. Beaumont, by suddenly saying, "Then there was not any truth in the report, which I have heard with horror, that you were going to marry Miss Beaumont to Sir John Hunter?"

"Then there was not any truth in the report I heard with horror, that you were going to marry yourself to a Spanish nun?" said Mrs. Beaumont, who had learned from a veteran in public warfare, that the best way to parry an attack is not to defend, but to make an assault.

"My dear Captain Walsingham," added she, with an arch smile, "I really thought you were a man of too much sense, and above all, too much courage, to be terror-struck by every idle report. You should leave such horrors to us weak women—to the visionary mind. Now, I could not blame poor Amelia, if she were to ask, 'Then was there no truth in the report of the Spanish incognita?'—No, no," pursued Mrs. Beaumont, playfully, refusing to hear Captain Walsingham; "not to me, not to me, must your defence be made. Appear before your judge, appear before Amelia; I can only recommend you to mercy."

What a charming woman this Mrs. Beaumont would be, if one could feel quite sure of her sincerity, thought Captain Walsingham, as he followed the lady, who, with apparently playful, but really polite grace, thus eluded all further inquiry into her secret manoeuvres.

"Here, my dearest Amelia," cried she, "is a culprit, whom I am bringing to your august tribunal for mercy."

"For justice," said Captain Walsingham.

"Justice! Oh, the pride of the man's heart, and the folly! Who ever talks of justice to a woman? My dear captain, talk of mercy, or cruelty, if you will; we ladies delight in being called cruel, you know, and sometimes are even pleased to be merciful—but to be just, is the last thing we think of: so now for your trial; public or private, Captain Walsingham?"

"Public! as I am innocent."

"Oyes, oyes! all manner of men," cried Mr. Beaumont.

"The Spanish cause coming on!" cried Mr. Palmer: "let me hear it; and let me have a good seat that I may hear—a seat near the judge."

"Oh, you shall be judge, Mr. Palmer," said Amelia; "and here is the best seat for our good judge."

"And you will remember," said Mr. Beaumont, "that it is the duty of a good judge to lean towards the prisoner."

"To lean! No, to sit bolt upright, as I will if I can," said old Mr. Palmer, entering into the pleasantry of the young people as readily as if he had been the youngest man in the company. As he looked round, his good countenance beamed with benevolent pleasure.

"Now, sir captain, be pleased to inform the court what you have done, or mean to do, with a certain Spanish nun, whom, as it is confidently asserted in a letter from one of your own men, you carried off from her nunnery, and did bring, or cause to be brought, with you to England."

"My lord judge, will you do me the favour, or the justice, to order that the letter alluded to may be read in court?"

This was ordered, and done accordingly.

"My lord judge," said Captain Walsingham, "I have nothing to object to the truth of the main points of this story; and considering that it was told by a very young man, and a traveller, it contains but a reasonable share of 'travellers' wonders.' Considering the opportunity and temptation for embellishments afforded by such a romantic tale, less has been added to it by the narrator than the usual progress of strange reports might have prepared me to expect. It is most true, as it has been stated, that I did, by her own desire, carry away from a nunnery, at —, this lady, who was neither a nun nor a Spanish lady, nor, as I am compelled by my regard to truth to add, young, nor yet handsome. My lord judge, far be it from me to impeach the veracity of the letter-writer. It is admitted by the highest and the lowest authorities, that beauty is a matter of taste, and that for taste there is no standard; it is also notorious, that to a sailor every woman is fair and young, who is not as old as Hecuba, or as ugly as Caifacaratadaddera. I can therefore speak only to my own opinion and judgment. And really, my lord, it grieves me much to spoil the romance, to destroy the effect of a tale, which might in future serve for the foundation of some novel, over which belles and beaux, yet unborn, might weep and wonder: it grieves me much, I say, to be compelled by the severity of this cross-examination to declare the simple truth, that there was no love in the case; that, to the very best of my belief and judgment, the lady was not in love with any body, much less with me."

"As you have admitted, sir," said the judge, "as you have voluntarily stated, that to a sailor every woman is fair and young, who is not as old as Hecuba, or as ugly as that other woman with the unspeakable name, you will be pleased to inform the court how it happened, or how it was possible, that in the course of a long voyage, you could avoid falling in love with the damsel whom you had thus rescued and carried off. Experience shows us, sir, that at land, and, I presume, at sea, proximity is one of the most common causes of love. Now, I understand, she was the only woman you saw for some months; and she had, I think you allow, possession of your cabin, to and from which you had of course constant egress and regress. Sir, human nature is human nature; here is temptation, and opportunity, and circumstantial evidence enough, in our days, to hang a man. What have you to offer in your defence, young man?"

"The plain fact, my lord, is, that instead of three months, I was but three days in the dangerous state of proximity with the Spanish lady. But had it been three months, or three years, there is my defence, my lord," said Captain Walsingham, bowing to Amelia. "At the first blush, you allow it, I see, to be powerful; but how powerful, you cannot feel as I do, without having looked, as I have done, into the mind."

"I have looked into the mind as well as you, sir. You have a great deal of assurance, to tell me I cannot feel and judge as well as you can. But, nevertheless, I shall do you justice. I think your defence is sufficient. I believe we must acquit him. But, pray—the plain matter of fact, which I wanted to hear, I have not yet got at. What have you done with this lady? and where is she?"

"She was carried safely to her friends—to her friend, for she has but one friend, that I could find out, an old aunt, who lives in an obscure lodging, in a narrow street, in London."

"And, upon honour, this is all you know about her?" said Mrs. Beaumont.

"All—except that she is in hopes of recovering some property, of which she says she has been unjustly defrauded by some of her relations. After I had paid my respects at the Admiralty, I made it my business to see the lady, and to offer my services; but into her lawsuits, I thank God, it was not my business to inquire, I recommended to her a good honest lawyer, and came here as fast as horses could carry me."

"But was not there some giving of diamonds, and exchanging of rings, one day, upon deck?" said Mrs. Beaumont.

"None," said Captain Walsingham; "that was a mere fable of poor Birch's imagination. I recollect the lady showed me a Spanish motto upon her ring; that is all I can remember about rings.—She had no diamonds, and very few clothes. Now," cried Captain Walsingham, growing a little impatient of the length of his trial, for he had not yet been able to speak for more than an instant to Amelia, "now, I hope, my trial is ended; else its length will be, as in some other cases, the worst of punishments."

"Acquitted! acquitted! honourably acquitted!" said Mr. Palmer.

"Acquitted, acquitted, honourably acquitted by general acclamation," cried Mr. Beaumont.

"Acquitted by a smile from Amelia, worth all our acclamations," said Mrs. Beaumont.

"Captain Walsingham," said Miss Hunter, "did the lady come to England and go to London in a Spanish dress and long waist?"

She spoke, but Captain Walsingham did not hear her important question. She turned to repeat it, but the captain was gone, and Amelia with him.

"Bless me! how quick! how odd!" said Miss Hunter, with a pouting look, which seemed to add—nobody carries me off!

Mr. Beaumont looked duller than was becoming.

Mrs. Beaumont applied herself to adjust the pretty curls of Miss Hunter's hair; and Mr. Palmer, in one of his absent fits, hummed aloud, as he walked up and down the room,

"'And it's, Oh! what will become of me?
Oh! what shall I do?
Nobody coming to marry me,
Nobody coming to woo.'"

CHAPTER XV

"True love's the gift which God has giv'n
To man alone, beneath the heav'n;
It is the secret sympathy,
The silver link, the silken tie,
Which heart to heart, and mind to mind,
In body and in soul can bind."

Happy love, though the most delightful in reality, is the most uninteresting in description; and lovers are proverbially bad company, except for one another: therefore we shall not intrude on Captain Walsingham and Amelia, nor shall we give a journal of the days of courtship; those days which, by

Rousseau, and many people, have been pronounced to be the happiest; by others, the only happy days of existence; and which, by some privileged or prudent few, have been found to be but the prelude to the increasing pleasures of domestic union.

Now that Mr. Beaumont saw his sister and his friend thus gratified in their mutual esteem and affection,—now that he saw all obstacles to their union removed, he became uncontrollably impatient to declare his own attachment to Miss Walsingham.

"My dear mother, I can bear it no longer. Believe me, you are mistaken in the whole romance you have imagined to yourself about Miss Hunter. She is no more in love with me than I am with her. Since you fixed my attention upon her, I have studied the young lady. She is not capable of love: I don't mean that she is not capable of wishing to be married, but that is quite a different affair, which need not give me any peculiar disturbance. My dear mother, find another husband for her, and my life for it, her heart will not break; especially if you give her bales of wedding finery enough to think and talk about for a calendar year.

"You abominably malicious monster of cruelty, I will not smile, nor will I allow you to indulge your humour in this manner at the expense of your poor victim."

"Victim! never saw a girl look less like a victim, except, indeed, as to her ornaments. I believe it is the etiquette for victims to appear dressed out with garlands, and ribands, and flowers."

"Positively, Edward, I won't allow you to go on in this style;—do you know you seriously hurt and offend me? do you consider that Miss Hunter's mother was my most intimate friend, and this match I have anxiously wished, in consequence of an agreement made between us at your birth and Albina's?"

"Oh, ma'am, those agreements never turned out well, from the time of the Arabian tales to the present moment. And you must pardon me if, after having tried all that reason and patience would do, in vain, I now come to impatience, and a little innocent ridicule. Except by laughing, I have no other way left of convincing you that I never can or will marry this young lady."

"But so pretty a creature! Surely you have thought her pretty."

"Extremely pretty. And I acknowledge that there have been moments when the influence of her—beauty, I can't call it—prettiness, joined to the power of my mother's irresistible address, have almost lapped me in elysium—a fool's paradise. But, thank Heaven and Miss Walsingham! I unlapped myself; and though the sweet airs took my fancy, they never imprisoned my soul."

"Vastly poetical! quite in the blue-stocking style."

"Blue-stocking! Dear mother, that expression is not elegant enough for you. That commonplace taunt is unworthy of my mother," said Mr. Beaumont, warmly, for he was thrown off his guard by the reflection implied on Miss Walsingham. "Ignorant silly women may be allowed to sneer at information and talents in their own sex, and, if they have read them, may talk of 'Les Précieuses Ridicules,' and 'Les Femmes Savantes,' and may borrow from Molière all the wit they want, to support the cause of folly. But from women who are themselves distinguished for talents, such apostasy—but I am speaking to my mother—I forbear."

"Great forbearance to your mother you have shown, in truth," cried Mrs. Beaumont, reddening with genuine anger: "Marry as you please! I have done. Fool that I have been, to devote my life to plans for the happiness and aggrandizement of my children! It is now time I should think of myself. You shall not see me the defeated, deserted, duped, despised mother—the old dowager permitted in the house of which she was once the mistress! No, no, Mr. Beaumont," cried she, rising indignantly, "this shall never, never be."

Touched and astonished by a burst of passion, such as he scarcely had ever before seen from his mother, Mr. Beaumont stopped her as she rose; and taking her hand in the most affectionate manner, "Forgive me, my dear mother, the hasty words I said just now. I was very much in the wrong. I beg your pardon. Forgive your son."

Mrs. Beaumont struggled to withdraw the hand which her son forcibly detained.

"Be always," continued he, "be always mistress of this house, of me, and mine. The chosen wife of my heart will never torment you, or degrade herself, with paltry struggles for power. Your days shall be happy and honoured: believe me, I speak from my heart."

Mrs. Beaumont looked as if her anger had subsided; yet, as if struggling with unusual feelings, she sat silent. Mr. Beaumont continued, "Your son—who is no sentimentalist, no speech-maker—your son, who has hitherto perhaps been too rough, too harsh—now implores you, by these sincere caresses, by all that is tender and true in nature, to believe in the filial affection of your children. Give us, simply give us your confidence; and our confidence, free and unconstrained, shall be given in return. Then we shall be happy indeed."

Touched, vanquished, Mrs. Beaumont leaned her head on her son, and said, "Then we shall be happy indeed!" The exclamation was sincere: at this moment she thought as she spoke. All her schemes were forgotten: the reversionary title, the Wigram estate—all, all forgotten: miraculous eloquence and power of truth!

"What happiness!" said Mrs. Beaumont: "I ask no other. You are right, my dear son; marry Miss Walsingham, and we have enough, and more than enough, for happiness. You are right; and henceforward we shall have but one mind amongst us."

With true gratitude and joy her son embraced her; and this was the most delightful, perhaps the only really delightful, moment she had felt for years. She was sincere, and at ease. But this touch of nature, strong as it was, operated only for a moment: habit resumed her influence; art regained her pupil and her slave! Captain Lightbody and Miss Hunter came into the room; and with them came low thoughts of plots, and notes, and baronets, and equipages, and a reversionary title, and the Wigram estate. What different ideas of happiness! Her son, in the mean time, had started up, mounted his horse, and had galloped off to realize some of his ideas of felicity, by the immediate offer of his hand to the lady who possessed his whole heart. Cool as policy, just recovered from the danger of imprudent sensibility, could make her, Mrs. Beaumont was now all herself again.

"Have you found much amusement shooting this morning, Lightbody?" said she, carelessly.

"No, ma'am; done nothing—just nothing at all—for I met Sir John in the grounds, and could not leave him. Poor Sir John, ma'am; I tell him we must get him a crook; he is quite turned despairing shepherd.

Never saw a man so changed. Upon my soul, he is—seriously now, Mrs. Beaumont, you need not laugh—I always told Sir John that his time of falling in love would come; and come it has, at last, with a vengeance."

"Oh, nonsense! nonsense, Lightbody! This to me! and of Sir John Hunter!"

Though Mrs. Beaumont called it, and thought it nonsense, yet it flattered her; and though she appeared half offended by flattery so gross, as to seem almost an insult upon her understanding, yet her vanity was secretly gratified, even by feeling that she had dependents who were thus obliged to flatter; and though she despised Captain Lightbody for the meanness, yet he made his court to her successfully, by persisting in all the audacity of adulation. She knew Sir John Hunter too well to believe that he was liable to fall in love with any thing but a fair estate or a fine fortune; yet she was gratified by feeling that she possessed so great a share of those charms which age cannot wither; of that substantial power, to which men do not merely feign in poetical sport to submit, or to which they are slaves only for a honey-moon, but to which they do homage to the latest hour of life, with unabating, with increasing devotion. Besides this sense of pleasure arising from calculation, it may be presumed that, like all other female politicians, our heroine had something of the woman lurking at her heart; something of that feminine vanity, which inclines to believe in the potency of personal charms, even when they are in the wane. Captain Lightbody's asseverations, and the notes Sir John Hunter wrote to his sister, were at last listened to by Mrs. Beaumont with patience, and even with smiles; and, after it had been sufficiently reiterated, that really it was using Sir John Hunter ill not to give him some more decisive answer, when he was so unhappy, so impatient, she at length exclaimed, "Well, Lightbody, tell your friend Sir John, then, since it must be so, I will consult my friends, and see what can be done for him."

"When may I say? for I dare not see Sir John again—positively I dare not meet him—without having some hope to give, something decisive. He says the next time he comes here he must be allowed to make it known to the family that he is Mrs. Beaumont's admirer. So, when may I say?"

"Oh, dearest Mrs. Beaumont," cried Miss Hunter, "say to-morrow."

"To-morrow! impossible!"

"But when?" said Miss Hunter: "only look at my brother's note to me again; you see he is afraid of being cast off at last as he was before about Amelia, if Mr. Palmer should object; and he says this disappointment would be such a very different affair."

"Indeed," said Captain Lightbody, "I, who am in Sir John's confidence, can vouch for that; for I have reason to believe, that—that the connexion was the charm, and that the daughter would not have been thought of. Stop, I was charged not to say this. But when Mrs. Beaumont, to return to my point—"

"Oh! name an early day," cried Miss Hunter, in a fondling tone; "name an early day for my brother's coming; and then, you know, it will be so nice to have the wedding days fixed for both marriages. And, dearest Mrs. Beaumont, remember I am to be your bride's-maid; and we'll have a magnificent wedding, and I shall be bride's-maid!"

"The dear innocent little creature, how mad she is with spirits! Well, you shall be my bride's-maid, if the thing takes place."

"If.—If to the winds!—Captain Lightbody, tell my brother—No, I'll write myself, and tell him he may come."

"How she distresses me! But she is so affectionate, one does not know how to be angry with her. But, my dear, as to naming the day when he may publicly declare himself, I cannot; for, you know, I have to break the affair to Mr. Palmer, and to my son and daughter, and I must take my own time, and find a happy moment for this; so name a day I cannot; but in general—and it's always safest to use general terms—you may say, soon."

This was Mrs. Beaumont's ultimatum. The note was written accordingly, and committed to the care of the confidential captain.

This business of mysterious note-writing, and secret negotiations5, was peculiarly suited to our heroine's genius and taste. Considering the negotiation to be now in effect brought within view of a happy termination, her ambassador, furnished with her ultimatum, having now actually set out on his ostensible mission of duck-shooting, our fair negotiatrix prepared to show the usual degree of gratitude towards those who had been the principal instruments of her success. The proper time, she thought, was now arrived, when, having no further occasion for Miss Hunter's services, she might finally undeceive her young friend as to any hopes she might retain of a union with Mr. Beaumont; and she felt that it was now indispensably necessary to disclose the truth, that her son had declared his attachment to Miss Walsingham.

Mrs. Beaumont opened the delicate case with a sigh, which claimed the notice of her young confidante.

"What a deep sigh!" said Miss Hunter, who was perfect, to use a musical term, in her lessons, pour observer les soupirs: "What a sigh! I hope it was for my poor brother?"

"Ah, no, my love! for one nearer my heart—for you."

"For me!—dear me!"

"You see before you a mother, all of whose fondest wishes and plans are doomed to be frustrated by her children. Amelia would have her way: I was forced to yield. My son follows her example, insists upon marrying without fortune, or extraordinary beauty, or any of the advantages which I had fondly pointed out in the daughter-in-law of my heart. You turn away from me, my darling! How shall I go on? how shall I tell you all the terrible truth?"

"Oh, ma'am, pray go on; pray tell me all."

"Miss Walsingham; that's all, in one word. These Walsinghams have forced themselves into my family,—fairly outwitted me. I cannot tell you how much, how deeply I am mortified!"

"Thank Heaven! I am not mortified," cried Miss Hunter, throwing back her head with pettish disdain.

Mrs. Beaumont, who had prepared herself for a fainting fit, or at least for a flood of tears, rejoiced to see this turn in the young lady's temper.

"That's right, my own love. Hew I admire your spirit! This pride becomes you, and is what I expected from your understanding. Set a just value upon yourself, and show it."

"I should set but little value on myself, indeed, if I did not think myself equal to Miss Walsingham; but Mr. Beaumont knows best."

"Not best, I fear," said Mrs. Beaumont; "but, from a child he was ever the most self-willed, uncontrollable being; there was no moving, no persuading him. There was no power, no appeal, my love, I did not try."

"Dear ma'am, I am excessively sorry you did."

"Why, my dear, I could not refrain from doing all I could, not only for my son's sake, but for yours, when I saw your affections, as I feared, so deeply engaged. But your present magnanimity gives me hopes that the shock will not be irrecoverable."

"Irrecoverable! No, really, ma'am. If Mr. Beaumont expects to see me wear the willow for him all my life, his vanity will be mistaken."

"Certainly, my dear," replied Mrs. Beaumont, "you would not be so weak as to wear the willow for any man. A young lady of your fortune should never wear the weeping but the golden willow. Turn your pretty little face again towards me, and smile once more upon me."

Miss Hunter had sat with her face turned from Mrs. Beaumont during the whole of this dialogue—"as if by hiding her face, she could conceal the emotions of her mind from me," thought her penetrating observer.

"Spare me, spare me, dearest Mrs. Beaumont," cried Miss Hunter, hiding her face on the arm of the sofa, and seeming now disposed to pass from the heights of anger to the depths of despair.

Mrs. Beaumont, less hard-hearted than some politicians, who care not who dies or lives, provided they attain their own objects, now listened at least with seeming commiseration to her young friend, who, with intermitting sighs, and in a voice which her position or her sobs rendered scarcely audible, talked of dying, and of never marrying any other man upon the earth.

Not much alarmed, however, by the dying words of young ladies, Mrs. Beaumont confined her attention to the absurdity of the resolution against marriage in general, and at this instant formed a plan of marrying Miss Hunter to one of her nephews instead of her son. She had one unmarried nephew, a young man of good figure and agreeable manners, but with only a younger brother's portion. To him she thought Miss Hunter's large fortune would be highly convenient; and she had reason to believe that his taste in the choice of a wife would be easily governed by her advice, or by her interest. Thus she could, at least, prevent her young friend's affections and fortune from going out of the family. In consequence of this glimpse of a new scheme, our indefatigable politician applied herself to prepare the way for it with her wonted skill. She soothed the lovelorn and pettish damsel with every expression that could gratify pride and rouse high thoughts of revenge. She suggested that instead of making rash vows of celibacy, which would only show forlorn constancy, Miss Hunter should abide by her first spirited declaration, never to wear the willow for any man; and that the best way to assert her own dignity would be to marry as soon as possible. After having given this consolatory advice, Mrs. Beaumont left the young lady's grief to wear itself out. "I know, my love," added she, "a friend of mine who would die for the happiness which my obstinate son does not, it seems, know how to value."

"Who, ma'am?" said Miss Hunter, raising her head: "I'm sure I can't guess whom you can possibly mean—who, ma'am?"

"Ah! my dear, excuse me," said Mrs. Beaumont, "that is a secret I cannot tell you yet. When you are 'fit to hear yourself convinced,' may be, I may obtain leave to tell you your admirer's name. I can assure you, he's a very fashionable and a very agreeable man; a great favourite with our sex, a particular friend of mine, and an officer."

"Lord bless me!" exclaimed Miss Hunter, starting quite up, "an officer! I can't imagine whom you mean! Dear Mrs. Beaumont, whom can you mean?"

Mrs. Beaumont walked towards the door.

"Only tell me one thing, dearest Mrs. Beaumont—did I ever see him?"

Mrs. Beaumont, wisely declining to answer any more questions at present, quitted the room, and left Miss Hunter dying—with curiosity.

The new delight of this fresh project, with the prospect of bringing to a happy termination her negotiation with Sir John Hunter, sustained Mrs. Beaumont's spirits in the midst of the disappointments she experienced respecting the marriages of her son and daughter; and enabled her, with less effort of dissimulation, to take apparently a share in the general joy which now pervaded her family. Her son expressed his felicity with unbounded rapture, when he found his proposal to Miss Walsingham graciously received by the object of his affections, and by all her family: his gratitude to his mother for no longer opposing his wishes gave a tenderness to his manner which would have touched any heart but that of a politician. Amelia, also, even in the midst of her love for Captain Walsingham, was anxiously intent upon showing dutiful attention to her mother, and upon making her some amends for the pain she had caused her of late. Whenever the brother and sister were together, in all their views of future happiness their mother was one of their principal objects; and these dispositions both Miss Walsingham and Captain Walsingham were earnest to confirm. No young people could have higher ideas than they had of the duty of children towards parents, and of the delight of family confidence and union. In former times, when Mr. Beaumont had been somewhat to blame in the roughness of his sincerity towards his mother, and when he had been disposed to break from her artful restraints, Captain Walsingham, by his conversation, and by his letters, had always used his power and influence to keep him within bounds; and whenever he could do so with truth, to raise Mrs. Beaumont in his opinion. She now appeared in a more advantageous light to her family, and they were more disposed to believe in her sincerity than they had ever been since the credulous days of childhood. The days of love and childhood are perhaps, in good minds, almost equally credulous, or, at least, confiding. Even Mr. Walsingham was won over by the pleasure he felt in the prospect of his daughter's happiness; and good Mr. Palmer was ten times more attentive than ever to Madam Beaumont. In his attention, however, there was something more ceremonious than formerly; it was evident, for he was too honest to conceal his feelings, that his opinion of her was changed, and that his attention was paid to her rather as the widow of his old friend than on her own account. Amelia, who particularly remarked this change, and who feared that it must be severely painful to her mother, tried by every honest art of kindness to reinstate her in his regard. Amelia, however, succeeded only in raising herself in his esteem.

"Do not disturb yourself, my dear young lady," said he to her, one day, "about your mother and me. Things are on their right footing between us, and can never be on any other. She, you see, is quite satisfied."

Mrs. Beaumont, indeed, had not Amelia's quick sensibility with regard to the real affections of her friends, though she was awake to every external mark of attention. She was content, as Mr. Palmer before others always treated her with marked deference, and gave her no reason to apprehend any alteration in his testamentary dispositions. When settlements were talked of for the intended marriages, Mr. Palmer seemed to consider Mrs. Beaumont first in all their consultations, appealed for her opinion, and had ever a most cautious eye upon her interests. This she observed with satisfaction, and she was gratified by the demonstrations of increased regard from her son and daughter, because she thought it would facilitate her projects. She wished that her marriage with Sir John Hunter should appear well to the world; and for this reason she desired that it should seem to be liked by all her family—seem, for as to their real opinions she was indifferent.

Things were in this situation, when Mrs. Beaumont caused herself to be surprised6 one morning by Mr. Palmer, with a letter in her hand, deep in reverie.

"Oh! my dear Mr. Palmer, is it you?" cried she, starting very naturally; "I was really so lost in thought—"

Mr. Palmer hoped that he did not disturb her.—"Disturb me! no, my good friend, you are the very person I wished to consult." Her eye glanced again and again upon the letter she held in her hand, but Mr. Palmer seemed provokingly destitute of curiosity; he however took a chair, and his snuff-box, and with a polite but cold manner said he was much honoured by her consulting him, but that of course his judgment could be of little service to a lady of Mrs. Beaumont's understanding.

"Understanding! Ah!" said she, "there are cases where understanding is of no use to women, but quite the contrary."

Mr. Palmer did not contradict the assertion, nor did he assent to it, but waited, with a pinch of snuff arrested in its way, to have the cases specified.

"In love affairs, for instance, we poor women," said Mrs. Beaumont, looking down prettily; but Mr. Palmer afforded no assistance to her bashful hesitation; she was under the necessity of finishing her sentence, or of beginning another, upon a different construction. The latter was most convenient, and she took a new and franker tone:—"Here's a letter from poor Sir John Hunter."

Mr. Palmer still sat bending forward to listen with the most composed deference, but pressed not in the slightest degree upon her confidence by any question or look down towards the letter, or up towards the lady's face, but straightforward looked he, till, quite provoked by his dulness, Mrs. Beaumont took the matter up again, and, in a new tone, said, "To be candid with you, my dear friend, this is a subject on which I feel some awkwardness and reluctance in speaking to you—for of all men breathing, I should in any important action of my life wish for your approbation; and yet, on the present occasion, I fear, and so does Sir John, that you will utterly disapprove of the match."

She paused again, to be asked—What match? But compelled by her auditor's invincible silence to make out her own case, she proceeded: "You must know, my good sir, that Sir John Hunter is, it seems, unconquerably bent upon a connexion with this family; for being refused by the daughter, he has proposed for the mother!"

"Yes," said Mr. Palmer, bowing.

"I thought you would have been more surprised," said Mrs. Beaumont: "I am glad the first sound of the thing does not, as I was afraid it would, startle or revolt you."

"Startle me, it could not, madam," said Mr. Palmer, "for I have been prepared for it some time past."

"Is it possible? And who could have mentioned it to you—Captain Lightbody?"

"Captain Lightbody!" cried Mr. Palmer, with a sudden flash of indignation: "believe me, madam, I never thought of speaking to Captain Lightbody of your affairs, I am not in the habit of listening to such people."

"But still, he might have spoken."

"No, madam, no; he would not have dared to bring me secret information."

"Honourable! quite honourable! But then, my dear sir, how came you to know the thing?"

"I saw it. You know, madam, those who stand by always see more than the players."

"And do you think my son and daughter, and Captain Walsingham, know it too?"

"I fancy not; for they have not been standers by: they have been deeply engaged themselves."

"That's well—for I wished to have your opinion and advice in the first place, before I hinted it even to them, or any one else living. As I feared the match would not meet your approbation, I told Sir John so, and I gave him only a provisional consent."

"Like the provisional consent of that young Irish lady," said Mr. Palmer, laughing, "who went through the marriage service with her lover, adding at the end of each response, 'provided my father gives his consent.'7 But, madam, though I am old enough certainly to be your father, yet even if I had the honour to be so in reality, as you are arrived at years of discretion, you know you cannot need my consent."

"But seriously, my excellent friend," cried she, "I never could be happy in marrying against your approbation. And let me, in my own vindication, explain to you the whole of the affair."

Here Mr. Palmer, dreading one of her long explanations, which he knew he should never comprehend, besought her not to invest him with the unbecoming character of her judge. He represented that no vindication was necessary, and that none could be of any use. She however persisted in going through a sentimental defence of her conduct. She assured Mr. Palmer, that she had determined never to marry again; that her inviolable respect for her dear Colonel Beaumont's memory had induced her to persist in this resolution for many years. That motives of delicacy and generosity were what first prevailed with her to listen to Sir John's suit; and that now she consoled and supported herself by the proud reflection, that she was acting as her dear Colonel Beaumont himself, could he know the circumstances and read her heart, would wish and enjoin her to act.

Here a smile seemed to play upon Mr. Palmer's countenance; but the smile had vanished in an instant, and was followed by a sudden gush of tears, which were as suddenly wiped away; not, however, before they reminded Mrs. Beaumont to spread her handkerchief before her face.

"Perhaps," resumed she, after a decent pause, "perhaps I am doing wrong with the best intentions. Some people think that widows should never, on any account, marry again, and perhaps Mr. Palmer is of this opinion?"

"No, by no means," said Mr. Palmer; "nor was Colonel Beaumont. Often and often he said in his letters to me, that he wished his wife to marry again after he was gone, and to be as happy after his death as she had been during his life. I only hope that your choice may fulfil—may justify—" Mr. Palmer stopped again, something in Shakspeare, about preying on garbage, ran in his head; and, when Mrs. Beaumont went on to some fresh topics of vindication, and earnestly pressed for his advice, he broke up the conference by exclaiming, "'Fore Jupiter, madam, we had better say nothing more about the matter; for, after all, what can the wit of man or woman make of it, but that you choose to marry Sir John Hunter, and that nobody in the world has a right to object to it? There is certainly no occasion to use any management with me; and your eloquence is only wasting itself, for I am not so presumptuous, or so unreasonable, as to set myself up for the judge of your actions. You do me honour by consulting me; but as you already know my opinion of the gentleman, I must decline saying any thing further on the subject."

Mrs. Beaumont was left in a painful state of doubt as to the main point, whether Mr. Palmer would or would not alter his will. However, as she was determined that the match should be accomplished, she took advantage of the declaration Mr. Palmer made, that he had no right to object to her following her own inclinations; and she told Sir John Hunter that Mr. Palmer was perfectly satisfied; and that he had indeed relieved her mind from some foolish scruples, by having assured her that it was Colonel Beaumont's particular wish, often expressed in his confidential letters, that his widow should marry again. So far, so good. Then the affair was to be broken to her son and daughter. She begged Mr. Palmer would undertake, for her sake, this delicate task; but he declined it with a frank simplicity.

"Surely, madam," said he, "you can speak without difficulty to your own son and daughter; and I have through life observed, that employing one person to speak to another is almost always hurtful. I should not presume, however, to regulate your conduct, madam, by my observations; I should only give this as a reason for declining the office with which you proposed to honour me."

The lady, compelled to speak for herself to her son and daughter, opened the affair to them with as much delicacy and address as she had used with Mr. Palmer. Their surprise was great; for they had not the most remote idea of her intentions. The result of a tedious conversation of three hours' length was perfectly satisfactory to her, though it would have been to the highest degree painful and mortifying to a woman of more feeling, or one less intent upon an establishment, a reversionary title, and the Wigram estate. How low she sunk in the opinion of her children and her friends was comparatively matter of small consequence to Mrs. Beaumont, provided she could keep fair appearances with the world. Whilst her son and daughter were so much ashamed of her intended marriage, that they would not communicate their sentiments even to each other,—they, with becoming duty, agreed that Mrs.

Beaumont was very good in speaking to them on the subject; as she had an uncontroulable right to marry as she thought proper.

Mrs. Beaumont now wrote letters innumerable to her extensive circle of connexions and acquaintance, announcing her approaching nuptials, and inviting them to her wedding. It was settled by Mrs. Beaumont, that the three marriages should take place on the same day. This point she laboured with her usual address, and at last brought the parties concerned to give up their wishes for a private wedding, to gratify her love for show and parade. Nothing now remained but to draw the settlements. Mrs. Beaumont, who piqued herself upon her skill in business, and who thought the sum of wisdom was to excel in cunning, looked over her lawyer's drafts, and suggested many nice emendations, which obtained for her from an attorney the praise of being a vastly clever woman. Sir John was not, on his side, deficient in attention to his own interests. Never was there a pair better matched in this respect; never were two people going to be married more afraid that each should take the other in. Sir John, however, pressed forward the business with an eagerness that surprised every body. Mrs. Beaumont again and again examined the settlements, to try to account prudentially for her lover's impatience; but she saw that all was right there on her part, and her self-love at last acquiesced in the belief that Sir John's was now the ardour of a real lover. To the lady's entire satisfaction, the liveries, the equipages, the diamonds, the wedding-clothes were all bought, and the wedding-day approached. Mrs. Beaumont's rich and fashionable connexions and acquaintance all promised to grace her nuptials. Nothing was talked of but the preparations for Mrs. Beaumont and Sir John Hunter's marriage; and so full of business and bustle, and mysteries, and sentimentalities, and vanities was she, that she almost forgot that any body was to be married but herself. The marriages of her son and daughter seemed so completely to merge in the importance and splendour of her own, that she merely recollected them as things that were to be done on the same day, as subordinate parts that were to be acted by inferior performers, whilst she should engross the public interest and applause. In the mean time Miss Hunter was engaged, to Mrs. Beaumont's satisfaction and her own, in superintending the wedding-dresses, and in preparing the most elegant dress imaginable for herself, as bride's-maid. Now and then she interrupted these occupations with sighs and fits of pretty sentimental dejection; but Mrs. Beaumont was well convinced that a new lover would soon make her forget her disappointment. The nephew was written to, and invited to spend some time with his aunt, immediately after her marriage; for she determined that Miss Hunter should be her niece, since she could not be her daughter. This secondary intrigue went on delightfully in our heroine's imagination, without interfering with the main business of her own marriage. The day, the long-expected day, that was to crown all her hopes, at length arrived.

CHAPTER XVI

"On peut étre plus fin qu'un autre, mais pas plus fin que tous les autres."
—ROCHEFOUCAULT.

The following paragraph extracted from the newspapers of the day, will, doubtless, be acceptable to a large class of readers.

"FASHIONABLE HYMENEALS.

"Yesterday, Sir John Hunter, of Hunter Hall, Devonshire, Bart., led to the hymeneal altar the accomplished Mrs. Beaumont, relict of the late Colonel Beaumont, of Beaumont Park. On the same day her son and daughter were also married—Mr. Beaumont to Miss Walsingham, daughter of E. Walsingham, Esq., of Walsingham House;—and Miss Beaumont to Captain Walsingham of the navy, a near relation of Edward Walsingham, Esq., of Walsingham House.

"These nuptials in the Beaumont family were graced by an overflowing concourse of beauty, nobility, and fashion, comprehending all the relations, connexions, intimate friends, and particular acquaintances of the interesting and popular Mrs. Beaumont. The cavalcade reached from the principal front of the house to the south gate of the park, a distance of three-quarters of a mile. Mrs. Beaumont and her daughter, two lovely brides, in a superb landau, were attired in the most elegant, becoming, fashionable, and costly manner, their dress consisting of the finest lace, over white satin. Mrs. Beaumont's was point lace, and she was also distinguished by a long veil of the most exquisite texture, which added a tempered grace to beauty in its meridian. In the same landau appeared the charming brides'-maids, all in white, of course. Among these, Miss Hunter attracted particular attention, by the felicity of her costume. Her drapery, which was of delicate lace, being happily adapted to show to the greatest advantage the captivating contour of her elegant figure, and ornamented with white silk fringe and tassels, marked every airy motion of her sylph-like form.

"The third bride on this auspicious day was Miss Walsingham, who, with her father and bride's-maids, followed in Mr. Walsingham's carriage. Miss Walsingham, we are informed, was dressed with simple elegance, in the finest produce of the Indian loom; but, as she was in a covered carriage, we could not obtain a full view of her attire. Next to the brides' equipages, followed the bridegrooms'. And chief of these Sir John Hunter sported a splendid barouche. He was dressed in the height of the ton, and his horses deserved particular admiration. After Sir John's barouche came the equipage belonging to Mr. Beaumont, highly finished but plain: in this were the two bridegrooms, Mr. Beaumont and Captain Walsingham, accompanied by Mr. Palmer (the great West-Indian Palmer), who, we understand, is the intimate friend and relative of the Beaumont family. Then followed, as our correspondent counted, above a hundred carriages of distinction, with a prodigious cavalcade of gentry. The whole was closed by a long line of attendants and domestics. The moment the park gates were opened, groups of young girls of the Beaumont tenantry, habited in white, with knots of ribands, and emblematical devices suited to the occasion, and with baskets of flowers in their hands, began to strew vegetable incense before the brides, especially before Mrs. Beaumont's landau.

'And whilst the priests accuse the bride's delay,
Roses and myrtles still obstruct her way.'

"The crowd, which assembled as they proceeded along the road to the church, and in the churchyard, was such that, however gratefully it evinced the popularity of the amiable parties, it became at last evidently distressing to the principal object of their homage—Mrs. Beaumont, who could not have stood the gaze of public admiration but for the friendly and becoming, yet tantalizing refuge of her veil. Constables were obliged to interfere to clear the path to the church door, and the amiable almost fainting lady was from the arms of her anxious and alarmed bride's-maids lifted out of her landau, and supported into the church and up the aisle with all the marked gallantry of true tenderness, by her happy bridegroom, Sir John Hunter.

"After the ceremony was over, Sir John and Lady Hunter, and the two other new-married couples, returned to Beaumont Park with the cortège of their friends, where the company partook of an elegant collation. The artless graces and fascinating affability of Lady Hunter won all hearts; and the wit, festive spirits, and politeness of Sir John, attracted universal admiration—not to say envy, of all present. Immediately after the collation, the happy couple set off for their seat at Hunter Hall.

"Mr. Beaumont, and the new Mrs. Beaumont, remained at Beaumont Park. Captain and Mrs. Walsingham repaired to Mr. Walsingham's.

"It is a singular circumstance, communicated to us by the indisputable authority of one of the bride's-maids, that Miss Walsingham, as it was discovered after the ceremony, was actually married with her gown the wrong side outwards. Whether this be an omen announcing good fortune to all the parties concerned, we cannot take upon us to determine; but this much we may safely assert, that never distinguished female in the annals of fashion was married under more favourable auspices than the amiable Lady Hunter. And it is universally acknowledged, that no lady is better suited to be, as in the natural course of things she will soon be, Countess of Puckeridge, and at the head of the great Wigram estate."

So ends our newspaper writer.

Probably this paragraph was sent to the press before the fashionable hymeneals had actually taken place. This may in some measure account for the extraordinary omissions in the narrative. After the three marriages had been solemnized, just when the ceremony was over, and Lady Hunter was preparing to receive the congratulations of the brilliant congregation, she observed that the clergyman, instead of shutting his book, kept it open before him, and looked round as if expecting another bride. Mrs. Beaumont, we should say Lady Hunter, curtsied to him, smiled, and made a sign that the ceremony was finished; but at this instant, to her astonishment, she saw her bride's-maid, Miss Hunter, quit her place, and beheld Captain Lightbody seize her hand, and lead her up towards the altar. Lady Hunter broke through the crowd that was congratulating her, and reaching Miss Hunter, drew her hack forcibly, and whispered, "Are you mad, Miss Hunter? Is this a place, a time for frolic? What are you about?"

"Going to be married, ma'am! following your ladyship's good example," answered her bride's-maid, flippantly,—at the same time springing forward from the detaining grasp, regardless even of the rent she made in her lace dress, she hurried, or was hurried on by Captain Lightbody.

"Captain Lightbody!" cried Lady Hunter; but, answering only with a triumphant bow, he passed on with his bride.

"Heavens! will nobody stop him?" cried Lady Hunter, over-taking them again as they reached the steps. She addressed herself to the clergyman. "Sir, she is a ward in chancery, and under my protection: they have no licence; their banns have not been published: you cannot, dare not, surely, marry them?"

"Pardon me, Lady Hunter," said Captain Lightbody; "I have shown Mr. Twigg my licence."

"I have seen it—I thought it was with your ladyship's knowledge," replied Mr. Twigg. "I—I cannot object—it would be at my own peril. If there is any lawful impediment, your ladyship will make it at the proper response."

A friend of Captain Lightbody's appeared in readiness to give the young lady away.

"The ceremony must go on, madam," said the clergyman.

"At your peril, sir!" said Lady Hunter. "This young lady, is a ward of chancery, and not of age!"

"I am of age—of age last month," cried the bride.

"Not till next year."

"Of age last month. I have the parish register," said Captain Lightbody. "Go on, sir, if you please."

"Good Heavens! Miss Hunter, can you bear," said Lady Hunter, "to be the object of this indecent altercation? Retire with me, and only let me speak to you, I conjure you!"

No—the young lady stood her ground, resolute to be a bride.

"If there is any lawful impediment, your ladyship will please to make it at the proper response," said the chaplain. "I am under a necessity of proceeding."

The ceremony went on.

Lady Hunter, in high indignation, retired immediately to the vestry-room with her bridegroom. "At least," cried she, throwing herself upon a seat, "it shall never be said that I countenanced, by my presence, such a scandalous marriage! Oh! Sir John Hunter, why did you not interfere to save your own sister?"

"Save her! Egad, she did not choose to be saved. Who can save a woman that does not choose it? What could I do? Is not she your ladyship's pupil?—he! he! he! But I'll fight the rascal directly, if that will give you any satisfaction."

"And he shall have a lawsuit too for her fortune!" said Lady Hunter; "for she is not of age. I have a memorandum in an old pocket book. Oh! who would have thought such a girl could have duped me so!"

Lady Hunter's exclamations were interrupted by the entrance of her son and daughter, who came to offer what consolation they could. The brilliant congregation poured in a few minutes afterwards, with their mingled congratulations and condolence, eager, above all things, to satisfy their curiosity.

Captain Lightbody, with invincible assurance, came up just as Lady Hunter was getting into her carriage, and besought permission to present his bride to her. But Lady Hunter, turning her back upon him without reply, said to her son, "If Captain Lightbody is going to Beaumont Park, I am not going there."

Mrs. Lightbody, who was now emancipated from all control, and from all sense of propriety, called out from her own carriage, in which she was seated, "That, thank Heaven! she had a house of her own to go to, and that nothing was farther from her thoughts than to interrupt the festivities of Lady Hunter's more mature nuptials."

Delighted with having made this tart answer, Mrs. Lightbody ordered her husband to order her coachman to drive off as fast as possible. The captain, by her particular desire, had taken a house for her at Brighton, the gayest place she could think of. We leave this amiable bride rejoicing in the glory of having duped a lady of Mrs. Beaumont's penetration; and her bridegroom rejoicing still more in the parish register, by the help of which he hoped to obtain full enjoyment of what he knew to be his bride's most valuable possession—her portion, and to defy Lady Hunter's threatened lawsuit.

In the mean time, Lady Hunter, in her point lace and beautiful veil, seated beside her baronet, in his new barouche, endeavoured to forget this interruption of her triumph. She considered, that though Miss Hunter's fortune was lost to her family, yet the title of countess, and the Wigram estate, were secure: this was solid consolation; and recovering her features from their unprecedented discomposure, she forced smiles and looks suitable to the occasion, as she bowed to congratulating passengers.

Arrived at Beaumont Park, she prepared, without appetite, to partake of the elegant collation, and to do the honours with her accustomed grace: she took care to seat Mr. Palmer beside her, that she might show the world on what good terms they were together. She was pleased to see, that though two younger brides sat near her, she engaged by far the largest share of public admiration. They were so fully content and engrossed by their own feelings, that they did not perceive that they were what is called thrown into the shade. All the pride, pomp, and circumstance of these glorious hymeneals appeared to them but as a dream, or as a scene that was acting before them, in which they were not called to take a part. Towards the end of the collation, one of the guests, my Lord Rider, a nobleman who always gave himself the air of being in a prodigious hurry, declared that he was under the necessity of going off, for he expected a person to meet him at his house in town, on some particular business, at an appointed day. His lordship's travelling companion, who was unwilling to quit so prematurely the present scene of festivity, observed that the man of business had engaged to write to his lordship, and that he should at least wait till the post should come in. Lady Hunter politely sent to inquire if any letters had arrived for his lordship; and, in consequence of his impatience, all the letters for the family were brought: Lady Hunter distributed them. There was one for Captain Walsingham, with a Spanish motto on the seal: Lady Hunter, as she gave it to him, whispered to Amelia, "Don't be jealous, my dear, but that, I can tell you, is a letter from his Spanish incognita." Amelia smiled with a look of the most perfect confidence and love. Captain Walsingham immediately opened the letter, and, looking at the signature, said, "It is not from my Spanish incognita,—it is from her aunt; I will read it by and by."

"A fine evasion, indeed!" exclaimed Lady Hunter: "look how coolly he puts it into his pocket! Ah! my credulous Amelia, do you allow him to begin in this manner?" pursued she, in a tone of raillery, yet as if she really suspected something wrong in the letter; "and have you no curiosity, Mrs. Walsingham?"

Amelia declared that she had none; that she was not one of those who think that jealousy is the best proof of love.

"Right, right," said Mr. Palmer; "confidence is the best proof of love; and yours, I'll venture to say, is, and ever will be, well placed."

Captain Walsingham, with a grateful smile, took his letter again out of his pocket, and immediately began to read it in a low voice to Amelia, Lady Hunter, and Mr. Palmer.

"DEAR SIR,

"Though almost a stranger to you, I should think myself wanting in gratitude if I did not, after all the services you have done my family, write to thank you in my niece's name and in my own: and much I regret that my words will so ill convey to you the sentiments of our hearts. I am an old woman, not well accustomed to use my pen in the way of letter-writing; but can say truly, that whilst I have life I shall be grateful to you. You have restored me to happiness by restoring to me my long-lost niece. It will, I am sure, give you satisfaction to hear, that my niece—"

Captain Walsingham stopped short, with a look which confirmed Lady Hunter in all her suspicions,—which made Mr. Palmer take out his snuff-box,—which startled even Mr. Beaumont; but which did not raise in the mind of Amelia the slightest feeling of doubt or suspicion. She smiled, and looked round at her alarmed friends with a manner which seemed to say, "Can you suppose it possible that there can be any thing wrong?"

"Pray go on, Captain Walsingham," said Lady Hunter, "unless—unless you have particular, very particular reasons."

"I have particular, very particular reasons," said Captain Walsingham; "and since," turning to Amelia, "this confiding lady does not insist upon my going on—"

"Oh!" said Lady Hunter, gaily, snatching the letter, "I am not such a credulous, or, as you call it, confiding lady."

"I beg of your ladyship not to read it," said Captain Walsingham, in an earnest tone.

"You beg of me not to read it, and with that alarmed look—Oh! positively, I must, and will read it."

"Not at present, then, I entreat you!"

"This very instant," cried Lady Hunter, affecting all the imperious vivacity of a young bride, under favour of which she determined to satisfy her malicious curiosity.

"Pray, Lady Hunter, do not read it," repeated Captain Walsingham, laying his hand over the letter. "It is for your own sake," added he, in a low and earnest voice, "it is for your own sake, not mine, that I beg of you to forbear."

Lady Hunter, imagining this to be only a subterfuge, drew the letter from beneath Captain Walsingham's hand, exclaiming, "For my sake! Oh, Captain, that is a charming ruse de guerre, but do not hope that it shall succeed!"

"Oh! mother, believe him, believe him," cried Amelia: "I am sure he tells you the truth, and he speaks for your sake, not for his own."

Amelia interceded in vain.

Mr. Palmer patted Amelia's shoulder fondly, saying, "You are a dear good creature."

"A dear credulous creature!" exclaimed Lady Hunter. She had now undisturbed possession of the letter.

Captain Walsingham stood by with a face of great concern; in which Amelia and Mr. Beaumont, without knowing the cause, seemed to sympathize.

The contest had early attracted the attention of all within hearing or view of her ladyship, and by this time had been pointed out and accounted for in whispers, even to the most remote parts of the room; so that the eyes of almost every individual in the assembly were now fixed upon Lady Hunter. She had scarcely glanced her eye upon the letter, when she turned pale as death, and exclaimed, "He knew it! he knew it!" Then, recollecting herself, she made a struggle to conceal her dismay—the forced smile quivered on her lip,—she fell back in a swoon, and was carried out of the room by her son and daughter. Sir John Hunter was at another table, eating eel-pie, and was the last person present who was made to understand what had happened.

"It is the damned heat of the room, I suppose," said he, "that made her faint;" and swallowing the last morsel on his plate, and settling his collar, he came up to Captain Walsingham. "What's this I hear?— that Lady Hunter has fainted? I hope they have carried her into the air. But where's the letter they say affected her so?"

"In my pocket," said Captain Walsingham, coolly.

"Any thing new in it?" said Sir John, with a sulky, fashionable indifference.

"Nothing new to you, probably, Sir John," said Captain Walsingham, walking away from him in disgust.

"I suppose it was the heat overcame Lady Hunter," continued Sir John, speaking to those who stood near him. "Is any body gone to see how she is now? I wonder if they'll let me in to see her."

With assumed carelessness, but with real embarrassment, the bridegroom went to inquire for his bride.

Good Mr. Palmer went soon afterwards, and knocked softly at the lady's door. "Is poor Lady Hunter any better?"

"Oh! yes; quite well again now," cried Lady Hunter, raising herself from the bed, on which she had been laid; but Mr. Palmer thought, as he saw her through the half-opened door, she still looked a deplorable spectacle, in all her wedding finery. "Quite well again, now: it was nothing in the world but the heat. Amelia, my love, go back to the company, and say so, lest my friends should be uneasy. Thank you, kind Mr. Palmer, for coming to see me: excuse my not being able to let you in now, for I must change my dress. Sir John sends me word his barouche will be at the door in ten minutes, and I have to hurry on my travelling dress. Excuse me."

Mr. Palmer retired, seeing clearly that she wished to avoid any explanation of the real cause of her fainting. In the gallery, leading from her room, he met Captain Walsingham, who was coming to inquire for Lady Hunter.

"Poor woman! do you know the cause of her fainting?" said Captain Walsingham.

"No; and I believe she does not wish me to know it: therefore don't tell it me," said Mr. Palmer.

"It is a secret that must be in the public papers in a few days," said Captain Walsingham. "This lady that I brought over from Lisbon—"

"Well, what can she have to say to Mrs. Beaumont?"

"Nothing to Mrs. Beaumont, but a great deal to Lady Hunter. You may remember that I mentioned to you that some of her relations had contrived to have her kept in that convent abroad, and had spread a report of her death, that the heir-at-law might defraud her of her property, and get and keep possession of a large estate, which fell to him in case of her death. Of further particulars, or even of the name of this estate, I knew nothing till this morning, when that letter from the aunt—here it is—tells me, that the estate to which her niece was entitled is the great Wigram estate, and that old Wigram was the rascally heir-at-law. The lawyer I recommended to the lady was both an honest and a clever fellow; and he represented so forcibly to old Wigram the consequences of his having his fraud brought to light in a court of equity, that he made him soon agree to a private reference. The affair has been compromised, and settled thus:—The possession of the estate is given up, just as it stands, to the rightful owner; and she forbears to call the old sinner to an account for past arrears. She will let him make it out to the world and to his own conscience, if he can, that he bona-fide believed her to be dead."

"So," said Mr. Palmer, "so end Madam Beaumont's hopes of being at the head of the Wigram estate, and so end her hopes of being a countess!—And actually married to this ruined spendthrift!—Now we see the reason he pressed on the match so, and urged her to marry him before the affair should become public. She is duped, and for life!—poor Madam Beaumont!"

At this moment Lady Hunter came out of her room, after having changed her dress, and repaired her smiles.

"Ready for my journey now," said she, passing by Mr. Palmer quickly. "I must show myself to the world of friends below, and bid them adieu. One word, Captain Walsingham: there's no occasion, you know," whispered she, "to say any thing below of that letter; I really don't believe it."

Too proud to let her mortification be known, Lady Hunter constrained her feelings with all her might. She appeared once more with a pleased countenance in the festive assembly. She received their compliments and congratulations, and invited them, with all the earnestness of friendship, to favour Sir John and her, as soon as possible, with their company at Hunter Hall. The company were now fast departing; carriages came to the door in rapid succession. Lady Hunter went through with admirable grace and variety the sentimental ceremony of taking leave; and when her splendid barouche was at the door, and when she was to bid adieu to her own family, still she acted her part inimitably. In all the becoming mixed smiles and tears of a bride, she was seen embracing by turns her beloved daughter and son, and daughter-in-law and son-in-law, over and over again, in the hall, on the steps; to the last moment contriving to be torn delightfully from the bosom of her family by her impatient bridegroom. Seated beside him in his barouche, she kissed her hand to Mr. Palmer,—smiled: all her family, who stood on the steps, bowed; and Sir John drove away with his prize.

"He's a swindler!" cried Mr. Palmer, "and she is—"

"Amelia's mother," interrupted Captain Walsingham.

"Right," said Mr. Palmer; "but Amelia had a father too,—my excellent friend, Colonel Beaumont,—whom she and her brother resemble in all that is open-hearted and honourable. Well, well! I make no reflections; I hate moral reflections. Every body can think and feel for themselves, I presume. I only say,—Thank Heaven, we've done with manoeuvring!"

Maria Edgeworth was born at Black Bourton, Oxfordshire on January 1st 1768, the second child of Richard Lovell Edgeworth and Anna Maria Edgeworth (née Elers).

Her early years were with her mother's family in England. Sadly, her mother died when Maria was only five. When her father married his second wife, Honora Sneyd, in 1773, the family went to live at his estate, Edgeworthstown, in County Longford, Ireland.

Maria was later sent to Mrs. Lattafière's school in Derby after Honora fell ill in 1775. There she studied dancing, French and other subjects. After Honora died in 1780 Maria's father married Honora's sister, Elizabeth, causing much social disapproved.

Maria transferred to Mrs. Devis's school in Upper Wimpole Street, London. Her father began to focus more attention on Maria in 1781 when she nearly lost her sight to an eye infection.

She returned home to Ireland at 14, and took charge of her younger siblings. She herself was home-tutored by her father in Irish economics and politics, science, literature and law. Despite her youth literature was in her blood.

She became her father's assistant in managing the Edgeworthstown estate, which had become run-down during the family's absence. Maria would now live and write there for the rest of her life.

With her father she began a lifelong academic collaboration. She meticulously detailed daily Irish life; a valuable lodestone of references for later use in her novels. Maria mixed with the Anglo-Irish gentry, and her aunt, Margaret Ruxton of Blackcastle, supplied her with the novels of Anne Radcliffe and William Godwin and encouraged her ambition to write.

Edgeworth's first published work in 1795 was 'Letters for Literary Ladies'. That same year 'An Essay on the Noble Science of Self-Justification', written for a female audience, states that the fair sex is endowed with an art of self-justification and women should use their gifts to continually challenge the force and power of men, especially their husbands, with wit and intelligence.

In 1796 her first children's book, 'The Parent's Assistant', which included the much loved short story 'The Purple Jar' was published.

In 1798 her father married for the fourth and last time, this time to Frances Beaufort. Frances was a year younger than Maria and they quickly became close.

'Practical Education' (1798) is a progressive work on education that combines the ideas of Locke and Rousseau with scientific inquiry. Edgeworth believed that "learning should be a positive experience and that the discipline of education is more important during the formative years than the acquisition of knowledge." The ultimate goal of Edgeworth's system was to create an independent thinker who understands the consequences of his or her actions.

Her first novel, 'Castle Rackrent' (1800) was published anonymously without her father's knowledge. It was an immediate success and firmly established Maria's appeal to the public.

'Belinda' (1801), was her first full-length novel. It dealt with love, courtship, and marriage, and she examined these as conflicts within her "own personality and environment; conflicts between reason and feeling, restraint and individual freedom, and society and free spirit." Startingly, 'Belinda' also included a depiction of interracial marriage between an African servant and an English farm-girl. Later editions of the novel, in line with unforgiving times, removed these sections.

Frances also pushed the family to travel more first London (1800), the Midlands (1802) and later the continent; first to Brussels and then to France. They met all the notables, with Maria even receiving a proposal of marriage from a Swedish courtier.

'Tales of Fashionable Life' (1809 and 1812) is a 2-series collection of short stories that often had its focus on the life of women. The second series was so successful that she was now the most commercially successful novelist of her age and ranked alongside her contemporaries Jane Austen and Sir Walter Scott.

On a visit to London in 1813, she met many notables including Lord Byron. She entered into a long correspondence with Sir Walter Scott after the publication of 'Waverley' in 1814, in which he acknowledged her influence, and they formed a lasting friendship. She visited him in Scotland at Abbotsford House in 1823 and the following year he visited Edgeworthstown.

After debating the issue with the economist David Ricardo, Maria came to believe that better management and the further use of science in agriculture would raise food production and help to lower prices. They were both in favour of Catholic Emancipation, enfranchisement for Catholics without property restrictions, agricultural reform and increased educational opportunities for women.

She worked particularly hard to improve the living standards of the poor in Edgeworthstown and to provide schools for the local children whatever their denomination.

After her father's death in 1817 she edited his memoirs, and extended them with her biographical addenda. Her father had married 4 times and sired 22 children. At the height of her creative endeavours, Maria had written, "Seriously it was to please my Father I first exerted myself to write, to please him I continued."

Maria worked for the relief of the famine-stricken Irish peasants during the Irish Potato Famine. She wrote 'Orlandino' and gave the proceeds to the Relieve Fund. However, during the famine her 'business head' insisted that only those tenants who had paid their full rent would receive any relief. She also punished any tenants who voted against her Tory preferences.

'Helen' (1834) is Maria Edgeworth's final novel, the only one she wrote after her father's death. Here the focus was on characters and situation and not moral lessons.

William Rowan Hamilton was elected president of the Royal Irish Academy and Maria's advice was constantly sought especially regarding literature in Ireland. She suggested that women should be allowed to participate in Academy events. Hamilton made Maria an honorary member in 1837.

After a visit to see her relations Maria was struck with severe chest pains and died suddenly of a heart attack in Edgeworthstown on 22nd May 1849. She was 81.

Maria Edgeworth is buried in the family tomb at St. John's Church, Edgeworthstown, Longford, Ireland.

Maria Edgeworth – A Concise Bibliography

Letters for Literary Ladies (1795) Second Edition (1798)
An Essay on the Noble Science of Self-Justification (1795)
The Parent's Assistant (1796)
Practical Education (1798) (2 Vols; collaborated with her father and step-mother)
Castle Rackrent (1800) Novel
Early Lessons (1801)
Moral Tales (1801)
Belinda (1801) Novel
The Mental Thermometer (1801)
Essay on Irish Bulls (1802)
Popular Tales (1804)
The Modern Griselda (1804)
Moral Tales for Young People (1805) (6 Vols)
Leonora (1806)
Essays in Professional Education (1809)
Tales of Fashionable Life (1809)
Ennui (1809) Novel
The Absentee (1812) Novel
Patronage (1814) Novel
Harrington (1817) Novel
Ormond (1817) Novel
Comic Dramas (1817)
Memoirs of Richard Lovell Edgeworth (1820) Editor
Rosamond: A Sequel to Early Lessons (1821)
Frank: A Sequel to Frank in Early Lessons (1822)
Tomorrow (1823) Novel
Helen (1834) novel
Orlandino (1848) Temperance novel